AGILE PROJECT MANAGEMENT

A BEGINNER'S GUIDE TO AGILE IMPLEMENTATION AND LEADERSHIP

JEREMY SAVELL

INTRODUCTION

There are specific systems that, once replaced, offer a new perspective on how businesses can conduct daily activities. Imagine the changes felt after the adoption of the telephone. Did it not completely shift how companies communicate internally, among each other, and with customers? How did a company culture and expectations change when decentralized information began flowing quickly?

Installing and adopting telephones required substantial investment upfront, both monetarily and with human capital. People needed to buy into the system and shift their expectations and understanding. But doing so guaranteed the continued existence of old companies, allowed new companies to ride the wake of the wave, and moved customer expectations of quality.

Now, technology is overwhelmingly available and easy to adopt. We can download new apps in under one minute; computers require hardware for every employee; and new technologies hold a shallow barrier to entry. The ability of a company to define a competitive advantage by means of the technologies it has is being undercut daily, while other technologies emerge. Not to mention that many of these functions are being further disrupted by the four elephants in the room: Apple, Facebook, Google, and Amazon can shift markets with a moment's notice, as they develop technologies that tower over the capabilities of other organizations.

Agile methodologies refer to how successful companies are fighting back. Agile is how they are winning. Rather than changing the tools used in the war, companies simply shift the way they *use* these tools. For example, look no further than Spotify's Scrum initiative. They are a decentralized group of teams fighting against Apple Music, Google Play, and Amazon Music at the same time—and they are winning. With less capital, fewer employees, and development capabilities, how can they do this? The answer is simple: they implemented Agile systems successfully.

Frustration has the power to permeate every aspect of life, to turn even the most optimistic men and women against systems they've reaped the benefits from for years beforehand. It demands change and adaptation. **The Agile Methodology of Project Management** was born from the collective frustration of seventeen professionals one night in Utah, in February 2001. Those thought leaders rewrote outdated and inefficient project management techniques with a clearer view in mind: to adapt and change with the world rather than attack new problems with old solutions. They called themselves the "Agile Alliance"— seventeen people who signed a brief, 68-word manifesto that would define project management in an ever-changing, digital world.

More than anything, the **Agile Manifesto** was a reaction to software projects falling apart for decades. Even before the 2001 software development world, requirements and opportunities were constantly shifting. Each member of the group was a leader of a software development team, some in different fields, all with various problems. There was one thing uniting them, though: their software projects rarely went particularly well. They had a brittle consistency to them that made it challenging to deliver a quality product on time, as expected. If a project did appear perfect, being clean, quick, and practical, it often ended up unused, over budget, and completely disorganized. Therefore, the team developed a better method. They moved their attention toward the customer, satisfying them beyond the perceived potential of the project. This approach minimizes lead times by the number of people touching the project, and each person who touches it makes the final product better. These projects were to have a certain sense of suave—everything was meant to flow toward success, as defined by functionality and timely delivery.

Just as software projects in 2001 struggled with orienting themselves to a changing and ever-shifting world, businesses and organizations today are experiencing the same issues. Projects span different business units and involve every aspect of an organization's capabilities, yet they are also associated with an increasingly early delivery date. The main principles of Agile address the main issue behind modern project management: rigidity. The source of this rigidity that defines current projects is threefold:

1. Reliance on Established Processes
2. Disconnected Expectations
3. Internal Team Hierarchy

The exploration of Agile systems goes beyond setting principles and ideas that the company can apply after a meeting or two. Agile systems are a paradigm shift in the culture, methods, and organization of a company. Each applied principle or law has the potential to modernize a company, dragging it into the future.

This book is about what that paradigm shift looks like on the ground and how you can take advantage of the Agile lessons promoted throughout modern software development organizations. Though this book focuses primarily on software application, it also looks at how we can apply these principles to different projects. If there is a hope to be more productive, deliver a working product consistently, satisfy a customer, and bring projects under budget, Agile principles may be what you need to meet all these goals.

Agile development has been in production since the 1960s, arguably even earlier than that, touched by some of the greatest minds in the world. It is an innate human ideal that spans beyond single industries in modernity. It extends from the successes of Rome and Alexander the Great in antiquity, to the first computer applications, and the modern reaction to exponential technological growth. That technological growth has enabled those same few companies to dominate the software development world in every fashion: from talent acquisition to production capabilities.

This piece will grant you a birds-eye view to the superpower that is Agile development, the tricks, and tools used over the years for successful implementation, and the descriptions of modern iterative models that have evolved from Agile version 1.0. From there, I encourage you to research more in-depth and contact an Agile coach to see if this approach is right for your organization or company. This book will not only grant you a deeper understanding of Agile principles and access to a new approach to project management; it will also give you a list of questions to consider while implementing Agile projects.

1

THE FLUID MANIFESTO

In 1985, Microsoft Excel 1.0 was released on Apple's Macintosh. After gaining notoriety and respect on the platform, Microsoft began developing a version for their systems. It took them two years to build the next Excel software for Windows, knowing they had a hit on their hands. They immediately began developing the second iteration of the software, Excel 3.0, which took three years. After 5.0 in 1993, Microsoft Excel became the default spreadsheet system for computers around the world. They seemed like an unstoppable juggernaut, releasing a new version again, in 1995. But what was actually going on behind the scenes?

Absolute *chaos*.

The chaos baffled a Microsoft employee named **Steve McConnell**. At the time, in 1998, he had been working at Microsoft for years and years, yet he could not understand the disorganization within the company. The first iteration of any project seemed to go swimmingly; lead times were accurate, product delivery was beautifully finished and in accordance with the specifications, and there were almost no complications outside the framework of the initial project. A team comprising only a few people could complete projects, and that at very little expense for the company. In time, things got complicated, though. Even if the definition itself had only shifted a little, the second iteration of the project took exponentially more people and money than the first; the third, even more so, and the following versions kept requiring more and more resources.

This reality perplexed Steve. The people at Microsoft were not unintelligent, so how was something so massive and significant as a software release consistently going so awry? In an attempt to clarify this question, Steve did some digging and learned a few things.

A few developers started working on the first iteration of a project, notably a software project, when they had an idea. In this example, we will use Tom and Jerry as the developers.

Tom and Jerry sit on their own, solving problems as they arise and developing solutions that immediately combat those problems. The issues they face are not only self-contained, but they only exist only between Tom and Jerry. Typically, they would produce the project in that environment, at a reasonable cost, on time, and with few complications. Then, success strikes—and everyone wants a piece.

So, they develop plans for the second project. This time, however, it isn't only Tom and Jerry working on the draft. The second version involves a vice president or two and maybe even a focus group. They all have their own opinions, but nothing seems to be excessively complicated in the early stages of the process. Tom and Jerry agree to incorporate these individuals' ideas into the final product. Three months into the project, however, the sales group comes through and asks for more storage capacity. Tom says, "That'll require additional functionality of the software, but we'll see what we can do." A few months later, the VP comes back with an idea that's *completely* different than the first one. The lawyers get involved and want to make the product satisfy the conditions of a new patent, and **Steve Ballmer** walks in asking where everyone is on the project.

Meanwhile, the delivery date keeps getting pushed forward, to the point of almost cancelling the project; three months, six months, a year even. The physical hardware, the customer's needs, and every aspect of the current project might differ from where it started. The expenses also exceed the first initiative by over *ten times,* while the product delivered is below standard and difficult to use.

Such a project, like many others, followed the traditional **WaterFall Method** of project management. It is an inherently stringent and restrictive method, that was too inflexible to address changes that occurred during the creation of a project. Instead of defining the problems with the system surrounding the development, Microsoft repeated the operation with every version, following an old-fashioned approach to project management.

The problems are not only related to how the software functions; instead, they refer to in how the software functions and satisfies the expectations of all the parties involved. What these people had previously experienced was tranquility; but what they got the next time around was chaos. The frustration with project management in the 1998 software world directly stemmed from situations like these. Modern projects continuously shift their focus toward the customer, but the underlying rigidity of organizations has remained constant, acting to deter the progress of a project.

It is important to note what Agile management systems *are not* before getting into what they actually *are.* Agile management is not standing up during a meeting, nor is it some grand idea a consulting company has exclusive access to. It does not exclude or forbid management involvement, nor is it a document-free system that inherently clashes with the existing ones.

The Agile Manifesto

Agile project management is the systematic breakdown of project rigidity through the utilization of Agile principles. It is a way of thinking that orients a project group toward inevitable change while preventing unnecessary human error. From its simplicity, flexibility arises. As if to exemplify this idea, the **Agile Manifesto** is a short 68 words long.

We are uncovering better ways of developing software by doing it and helping others do it. Through this work we have come to value:

Individuals and interactions over processes and tools

Working software over comprehensive documentation

Customer collaboration over contract negotiation

Responding to change over following a plan

That is, while there is value in the items on the right, we value the items on the left more.

These are not stringent rules to follow—they are a set of values. The Agile Manifesto precisely articulates precisely the focus of a project manager without disregarding the nuances of a situation. At the core of this Manifesto, the Agile Alliance created a set of values to "[promote] organizational models based on people, collaboration, and building the organizational communities in which [they] would want to work." These values rely on trust and collaboration, focusing on the people in the system rather than the analytics behind them.

Individuals and Interactions over Processes and Tools

Project processes and tools vary from project to project, and from company to company. The people implementing and abiding by those processes will always remain the consistent factor. The Agile Manifesto proposes a simple shift of focus from framing projects to the people executing them. Processes will rarely be a source of the innovation needed to address a changing list of problems. The already-established methods come with a certain rigidity and structure that make it difficult to evolve in line with the changes that happen during the life cycle of a project. This does not only make the final delivery underwhelming, but it also jeopardizes the productive potential of the entire project. As such, the Agile values came as a direct response to the WaterFall method, which had hoped to guarantee success through stringent phases. Rather than adhering to guidelines, the Agile approach requires *trust* in employees and small teams to solve problems with innovative solutions as they arise. The shift in focus is visible inasmuch as overreliance on processes and tools is replaced by the reliance on competent people who can react in time.

Specifically, when working with a WaterFall methodology, we would require substantial documentation before we ever built software. This meant a huge opportunity cost, led to extra and unused features being integrated into the software, and was highly ineffective at meeting customer needs. By contrast, this second value of the Agile method is simple: produce something that works. A focus of modern project management is the constant shifting of a project. From the resources available, the external and internal situations surrounding the project, and the stakeholders involved in the project, things change. The only certainty is that things will change—the farther a team is from the final delivery, the more likely it becomes that a shift will redefine the project altogether. Start moving; don't waste time. The goal of a project should always be **tangibility over theoretical concepts**: do not wait for the theoretical to become irrelevant. Having a tangible product allows for feedback and provides developers with the opportunity to make adjustments in real-time, within the context of the present logic and understanding. This is critical when developing any project, software or otherwise.

Customer Collaboration over Contract Negotiations

Customer centricity is a core functionality for the wellbeing of most businesses. When delivering a project, two lists must run parallel. The contract represents the first: "Is this what I, the Customer, ordered?" If the answer is yes, the business concludes, and they should receive a payment within 90 days. However, there is a second list: "Am I, the Customer, happy with this? Is this what I need?" Often, the needs a customer had when signing a contract shifted during the execution of the project. In the field of software engineering, this factor used to be heavily influenced by the need for more time. But even now, when it's possible for businesses to shift entire strategies from one week to another, the difference between the "What I Ordered" and "What I Need Upon Delivery" grows. And with that, as a customer-centric business, comes the need to shift expectations. The design of the Agile value is to change project managers' focus from the dotted line to actually putting the project within the customer's eyesight. This value asks project managers to take the customer with them on a journey rather than deliver at the final destination. It removes disappointment and surprise on the customer's side, while also allowing a team to adapt to customer needs, cut out excess work, and deliver a product that can be used more effectively.

Responding to Change over Following Plans

The old saying, "Failing to plan is planning to fail," has fallen out of style. This Agile value is not discriminating against the necessity of planning, blatantly suggesting that you should blatantly abandon it; instead, it puts forward the concept of a hierarchy. When the plan and reality come to a head, it is the project manager's job to recognize facts over the idea. This applies to daily life quickly—if a GPS screams "next right" into a construction zone, an intelligent driver adapts and searches for another route. The same philosophy works in our business-related affairs. any plan is likely to hit some unforeseen obstacle beyond the development scope of the project, because no company or project team can anticipate all macro and micro shifts in the business world. However, in Agile systems, obstacles are opportunities for change and increased overall value rather than things to barrel through for the sake of the original plan.

The Twelve Principles of Agile

The Agile Alliance did not stop at simply drawing up a plan with four values and then continuing with the ski trip. Based on these values, and driven by the snow-covered lodge in Utah, a set of twelve Principles was born.

---

1. Our highest priority is to satisfy the customer through early and continuous delivery of valuable software.

Think about how the function of a project shifts when its greatest beacon, its greatest goal, is something as simple as satisfying the customer. This principle proposed by the Agile Alliance is the first because it acts as a lighthouse for the others—everything else, if done correctly, follows this idea. This rule breaks down the hierarchical division within a team in one swoop. "Is this in the customer's service?" If so, it's a *Go*. If not, it's a hard *No*. This principle also emphasizes "early" and "continuous" delivery. Not only do these two characteristics allow for the specific development of new customer requirements, but they also impose continuous communication with the customer early on, while the direction of the project is more malleable, and allow clients to react to the tangible product in real-time. This idea is powerful for any project. Define the customer, work with them from the very beginning, on a continuous basis, and ensure their satisfaction through structured collaboration.

2. Welcome changing requirements, even late in development. Agile processes harness change for the customer's competitive advantage.

The "Agile" piece of Agile Management manifested from this idea of thriving within change. An Agile system not only expects change but reacts effectively and takes advantage of opportunities stemming from it. This echoes ideas surrounding empiricism, the principle of growing through senses and the world rather than through thought and planning. As the project is being built, both the team members developing the plan, and the customer will gain a better understanding of the project's potential and customer needs. An Agile organization focuses on delivering a product that will satisfy the customer, which will reveal necessary changes throughout the development process. These are a critical opportunity for their customer's business to move ahead effectively, and also for the organization to become irreplaceable by shifting expectations with the learning that happens during a project's development.

3. Deliver working software frequently, from a couple of weeks to a couple of months, with a preference to the starter timescale.

This is the medium that allows for the first two principles to exist at all! Frequent delivery of the product and product updates throughout the development process allows for a line of communication to exist parallel to development. This mitigates overall risk by enabling rapid, real-time feedback from the customer. By the time the project is ready for delivery, the customer knows exactly what they will receive/implement.

---

4. Business people and developers must work together daily throughout the project.

The more significant lesson this principle conveys is one of internal stakeholder unity. In the same way that Microsoft had different organizational leaders, business units, and internal corporate structures clashing with the final delivery, business people and developers have had traditionally strained relations. While keeping the customer in the loop is critical, a second piece of the puzzle refers to organizing internal stakeholders in such a way that they never lose their input, risking a delay or the creation of an unsatisfactory product. For most projects, this extends to not only to business leaders and developers, but also to anyone with the ability to influence the delivery date: lawyers, executives, internal business units etc.—everyone needs to be on the same page as to where the project has been, is, and will be. This ensures that every branch involved in the project, be it business, technical, legal, or organizational, is working to achieve the same delivery date.

---

5. Build projects around motivated individuals. Give them the environment and support they need, and trust them to get the job done.

Stemming directly from the first value, this principle delicately articulates the need for individuals to be the center of an Agile project. Running Agile requires the trust of these individuals, for these individuals will get the job done and create a better product than any other group of unmotivated or coerced employees. Find motivated people for the project to succeed and give them enough fuel to get there, whatever that might entail.

---

6. The most efficient and effective method of conveying information to and within a development team is face-to-face conversation.

Communication is a consistent issue within teams. With teams being increasingly remote and decentralized, this piece of the twelve is more and more challenging to uphold. However, its importance lies in the attention that comes from people communicating face to face. Many Agile teams work in an entirely decentralized manner. The sixth principle therefore articulates the concept of prioritization. While emails and text can be subject to ambiguity and misinterpretation, face-to-face conversation makes the organization more effective and efficient, while simultaneously minimizing the risk of miscommunication.

Another massive implication of this principle is the fifth —supporting the team. If the team needs the approval of an executive, advice from a legal team, or anything from anyone, they must have immediate access to a face-to-face conversation with that person. It is a manager's job to facilitate that access.

> 7. Working software is the primary measure of progress.

This is a direct echo of the second Value of Agile project management—providing working software. If a project team does not or cannot deliver a working product throughout the development process, they are not working in an Agile way. Furthermore, this principle highlights the notion that working software is the measure of progress, not completion itself. A functional expectation of an Agile project is for it to be consistently practical rather than ensure functionality upon delivery.

> 8. Agile processes promote sustainable development. The sponsors, developers, and users should be able to maintain a constant pace indefinitely.

Many of the organizations that fail at Agile implementation usually encounter difficulties at this stage—longevity. For something to be Agile, you cannot rush it or demand exhaustive efforts from the people involved. Implementing an Agile system should be in infinitum. Simple metric manipulation often tempts organizations that impose Agile principles on projects to demand faster, under-budget project delivery. If it forces salaried employees to hit a deadline by working overtime and as quickly as possible, a project can seem Agile; however, this is not sustainable and will lead to a breakdown in the team, undermining any other Agile principles introduced. Agile is durable, with a focus on endurance over project turnover.

9. Continuous attention to technical excellence and good design enhances agility.

This principle shifts project quality from task-oriented projects to a more artistic delivery. The mindset when approaching an Agile project should shift from "How is this done?" to "How can we do this better?" This shift is critical in software, as a means of creating and improving a product lie within the approach to code. Change becomes much more cumbersome throughout the life cycle of a project—applying this rule works to ensure that the focus of the team is uniform in the effort to produce a singular product.

10. Simplicity - the art of maximizing the amount of work not done - is essential.

Keep things simple. This applies to all aspects of a project, as preferences should be shifted. Keep teams small and projects focused. Measure progress using a few meaningful **key performance indicators** (**KPIs**) rather than over-measuring. Grant your team the power to move swiftly through the organization, avoiding roadblocks at every request. Even in the way we develop the product it is essential to organize resources in such a way that you do a few things very well rather than many things poorly. Keeping the aims and goals of the product in mind helps the team remain focused and deliver a useful product to the end-user. The methods for accomplishing simplicity should be unique to the project/the project team and inherently require both innovation and creativity from management.

---

11. The best architectures, requirements, and designs emerge from self-organizing teams.

Instill a **bottom-up approach** to project development! A part of the trust required in these project teams means handing the reins to responsible people. Direct questions to a group rather than make demands and point out faulty architecture—allow the members of the team to organize on their own, depending on the project at hand.

Having a team self-organize requires a different approach to their management. However, self-organized teams are more collaborative, competent, and motivated—creating that environment means establishing an invaluable asset within an Agile project.

---

12. At regular intervals, the team reflects on how to become more effective, then tunes and adjusts its behavior accordingly.

Last but not least, this principle calls for continuous improvement and self-evaluation. Inevitably, problems will arise and require attention. The Twelfth Principle concretely states the importance of constant reflection and process improvement within a team. This idea is fundamental to an Agile team, because they live in change—the performance of the project and the customer's satisfaction will directly affect any sense of rigidity throughout the organization.

Chapter One Summary

Let's review some of the key points from this first chapter.

- A uniform focus on customer satisfaction is paramount for Agile projects.
- Agile teams thrive in change—rigidity is the enemy of progress.
- Progress is defined by functional product delivery and feedback from the customer.
- Trust and respect for the team are requirements for fluidity and functionality.

The next chapter will outline the roots of the Agile approach to management, the overall benefits of the system, and a modern example of Agile systems executed successfully.

2

BEHIND AGILE

The Roman Empire was one of the greatest civilizations in history, spanning from the hills in the north of the modern-day United Kingdom all the way to the warmth of Northern Africa. The strength of the Roman Empire lies not only in its armies and wealth, but also in the system that enabled those to exist: roads. These roads were so critical to the structure and security of the Empire, both economically and militarily, that the Roman soldiers themselves got dispatched to maintain and develop these systems. The ones selected for the task were highly trained; they arguably made up the best army of their time and were put in charge of filling potholes and adding new lanes.

It was not uncommon for each member of the legion to have a specialty. This shifted from architects and engineers to butchers and ditch-diggers, anything needed to support construction or repair works, regardless of the project scale. In this context, it is important to note that many of the resulting constructions are still visible to modern onlookers; furthermore, some of them have lived on for centuries after nation that had created them collapsed.

It's no doubt that the veins of an empire, the systems

that allow a nation to thrive, are of the utmost importance. These allowed the armies to move around the empire and maintain order, encouraged trade to and from Rome and connected the nation as one. The people did not take the importance of a single bridge lightly, hence their persistence into the 21st century.

Imagine, though, that the army did not function properly. That no matter how well-trained, well-equipped, and determined the Roman Legionaries were to build a bridge that would last centuries, they never reached the other bank. Imagine if they took decades to make it, but it was still not sturdy enough to hold a person. That money was not an option, and regardless of the amount invested, most of the roads were unusable and left half-finished. If every road built led to nowhere instead of Rome, how long could a nation, whose existence relied almost entirely on their functionality, survive?

This was the state of software development between 1965 and 1985: broken bridges, roads leading to no destination, and mountains of dollars burned before everyone's eyes. The importance of functional software was heavily linked to the success or failure of a business, yet the software development industry could not deliver on projects, no matter the incentive. It was an industry in crisis.

Moreover, it was an industry stuck in the past. Even though there were many forms of software development processes before it, the WaterFall methodology appeared as the culmination of those older ideas. The development of functional software is not as concrete as that of a bridge, yet during those times, people applied a similar, if not identical, rationale to those new types of projects. For 35 years, the software development industry would develop Agile and Scrum principles. However, as those specific management styles highlight repeatedly, there were many iterations beforehand.

The Software Crisis

The difficulty proliferating throughout the software development community of the late 1960s was the answer to a single question: how can projects keep up with changes from every direction? In the impossibly famous paper by Edsger W. Dijkstra, titled *A Humble Programmer,* the issue is described as one stemming from technological shifts:

The major cause of the software crisis is that the machines have become several orders of magnitude more powerful! To put it quite bluntly: as long as there were no machines, programming was no problem at all; when we had a few weak computers, programming became a mild problem, and now we have gigantic computers, programming has become an equality gigantic problem.

Chaos seemed to be a way of life within the software industry. Projects ran overtime and over budget as the new normal. If the organization could deliver them at all—which was not a guarantee—they were often of poor quality, unusable, or irrelevant to the technology that would be released before their reinvestment could give them any competitive edge. The dilemma for businesses was impossible; a project that will take longer and cost more than expected would become useless or require replacement before it delivers its anticipated value, but without it, competitors would overrun the company.

The chaos persisted into the 1970s, when one man, **Dr. Winston Royce**, attempted to devise a solution: The WaterFall Method.

The Responses: WaterFall and Others

The Waterfall Method outlined a simple, logical set of processes that a company would need to follow for a project to be successful. Its name comes from the accompanying metaphor of water gently cascading down a predictable, steady, incremental stream. Royce outlined the life cycle of software development processes in **six simple steps**.

1. Requirements

What is the proposed final software product supposed to do? Typically, companies would answer this first question by writing a systematic, detailed document that would serve as the basis for all future developments.

2. Analysis

Further in the document, this layer involves more of the business in the development of the project. It generates models that executives consult, and ideally, the project receives the go-ahead at the end of the analysis process.

3. Design

At this stage, the technical requirements come into question. These include, but are not limited to, hardware specifications, programming language, data layers, and many more technical aspects of the project.

4. Code

Guided by the initial requirements, business specifications, and design framework, the software development begins here. It involves typing with little interaction or input from outside of those three starting frameworks. It is not uncommon for this stage to be repeated after the testing phase.

5. Testing

Beta program testers would prod and probe the application, looking for things that might need adjustment. If there are none, which is rarely the case, the project will pass onto the *Operations* stage. If there is room for adjustment, though, the project will regress to the coding stage so that the developers can improve or re-develop in the least intrusive manner possible.

6. Operations

This stage not only includes the live deployment of software into a system, but also refers to the maintenance and support that follow. The development of the software is complete, and all responsibilities of the implementing company shift to short-term bug repair or general patchwork.

FOR TEN YEARS, the WaterFall Method was the standard system in the software development universe. And for ten more years, the chaos persisted. Though Royce intended to help in project development, others manipulated his ideas to address a different issue. The WaterFall method was not used to tackle the realities behind software development, instead companies set out to address their need for control within said chaos. The Waterfall Method, at its core, allows for departmentalization and logical progression over an ever-changing set of constraints and systems. The strength of the system lies in its ability to work within the existing structures and political realities of a business—teams can shift, contracts can define successful delivery, and managers can point to specific, incremental metrics of accomplishment. Everyone wins...

Except for the customer, who receives inadequate or useless software *86% of the time a company uses the Waterfall Method for project management*. There are more than a few realities that the Waterfall Method did not address. Thankfully, there were thinkers in the early 80s who came onto the scene with fresh criticism, which in turn brought about better methodologies. These methodologies and philosophies lie at the core of modern Agile and Scrum methods.

Protests and Shifts (Hollywood, EVO, RIPP, RAD)

The most significant shifts from the WaterFall Method came in the late '70s and early '80s, from two directions. The Software Crisis was in full swing. Even then, after ten years of improvements, *75% of software development and projects were unused or never finished*. The first of these directions came incrementally, through modern interpretations of older ideas.

Iterations and Incremental Development (**IID**) was slowly proving to be a viable option for software development, but it was far from the obvious solution we see it as today. Various projects expressed IID differently, but the core functionality was consistent: develop short goals or small versions, test and prove them, then carry out further development.

In 1976, **Tom Gilb** published a paper titled "**Software Metrics**." In it, he not only coined the term "software metrics," he also reintroduced the lost hopes of the WaterFall Method with one word: evolution. Introducing this idea into the lexicon of software development was a first. With it, the core concept of iterations addressing the shifts within a project was set up. This idea shifted the focus from delegating responsibilities and the safety of resources to a more aggressive, acrobatic approach to iterative design.

What followed after this publication was a wave of experiments and process practices surrounding the theme of software project evolution through iteration, culminating in the landmark paper "**Iterations and Incremental Development: A Brief History**" by **Larman** and **Basili**. By 1980-1981, IID had exploded into the software development world.

Not long after, in 1982, **G. R. Gladden** attempted to address a different set of issues. In his view, there were three main critique points concerning the WaterFall Method as a functional project management tool that needed to be taken into consideration:

1. Requirements are often poorly thought out because the customer rarely knows what they need.
2. "The life cycle approach exacerbated that problem..." by creating "eleventh-hour alterations" to final products.
3. "The elapsed time between requirements and a

delivered product erodes a customer's confidence."

These three realities caused project delays, unhappy customers, overspending, and disastrous software implementations. Gladden, an engineer at heart, saw an opportunity for improvement and stepped into the mold with three concise propositions. With a sense of humor and understanding of cinema production, he created the **Non-Cyclical Hollywood Method**:

Prop 1: System objectives are more important than system requirements

Prop 2: Physical objects convey more information than written specifications

Prop 3: System objectives + Demonstration = Successful products

Do those sound familiar? These three would later turn into larger ideals and principles within the Agile Manifesto. But first, they would manifest in the precursors of Agile.

Gilb wasn't done with his influence on the software engineering world just yet, though. In 1985, with his paper **"Evolutionary Delivery v. the Waterfall Method,"** he described the **EVO method**. Birthed from many other pieces about new processes, this process is a conglomeration of new ideas and Gilb's fundamental laws, established in his 1975 paper. The EVO method holds true to three simple principles:

1. Deliver something real to the end-user.
2. Measure the added-value to the user in all critical dimensions.
3. Adjust both design and objectives based on observed realities.

With these ideas in mind, Gilb included eight critical concepts that explained his method. He attempted to redirect the focus of the software world. The EVO method was the first to a customer-facing software development project. All three principles were designed to incorporate customer options and place focus on the delivery of a high-quality, useful product. Gilb stressed this point consistently, saying:

With evolutionary delivery the situation is changed. The developer is specifically charged with listening to the user reactions early and often. The user can play a direct role in the development process.

Furthermore, he insisted they throw the focus on process orientation out the window altogether. Result orientation was the focus of an EVO project—a concept that other processes had seldom expressed until this point. Of process orientation, Gilb said:

Evolutionary delivery forces the developers to get outside of the building process for a moment, frequently and early - and find out whether their ship is navigating towards that port of call many cycles of delivery away.

The influence that this paper, and the shifts and future deployments it inspired, had upon the Agile process development cannot be stressed enough. These were the first changes toward consistent product delivery over documentation, customer orientation, and stress on finished products that the software development industry had experienced. Gilb's principles met Agile requirements and procedures almost entirely; however, the industry had just begun its journey toward Agile.

Three years later, in 1988, the **DuPont company** introduced a method called the **Rapid Iterative Production Prototyping** (**RIPP**). The company shocked the industry with a single claim: "Working software in 90 days... or your money back." This method later formalized and was expanded in 1991 by **James Martin**, who named his iteration **Rapid Application Development** (**RAD**).

RAD Methodology comprises four set phases: **requirement planning**, **user design**, **construction**, and **implementation**. These resemble other methodologies like EVO and even WaterFall, but what distinguishes RAD from those typical processes is its *scale*. The RAD process would not be applied to the larger project, but rather be used for compartmentalized transactions of functional software that the team would present to the final customer for input. This shift enables continuous iteration on a restricted time scale, blurring the lines between finished product and progression. The system relies heavily on these "**timeboxes**," which are exact periods of time devoted by a specific team to a single transaction, thus being consistent and manageable. RAD not only favors a high number of iterations, but it also redirects focus to the incremental production of the working product. If a team doesn't believe they can complete the task in the time provided, RAD philosophy argues that the organization needs to reduce the scope and add another transaction to the project. As such, RAD places emphasis on timeboxes and iterative delivery.

RAD was the last true precursor of the Agile Manifesto, as it fits almost entirely in the Agile framework except for its stringent timeframes. RAD also recommended small teams and quick delivery, bringing the industry another step closer to Agile.

Disorganized Agile Principles

University-sponsored papers did not describe all the methodologies in use eloquently, nor did companies market these methodologies as valid. Before the Agile Manifesto was signed and published, three other processes were defined in detail: **Extreme Programming** (**XP**), **Scrum**, and **Crystal**. Several people who faced similar problems in their field of expertise developed these three methodologies separately from each other. The three system creators developed and signed the Agile Manifesto, but where did their systems emerge from?

In 1991, IBM asked **Alistair Cockburn** to write a methodology paper on object-technology projects. With due diligence, Cockburn interviewed some of IBM's process teams and found a few discrepancies between their stories and what others had described in the literature. From these interviews, he gained a better understanding of how valuable communication, moral, and access to the end-user were to the successful implementation of a project. As the lead consultant on a $15M, fixed-scope project, with a 45-person team, Cockburn then carried out multiple experiments to verify his findings. The plan was successful, and his conclusions later led to the creation of the Agile Method **Crystal**. Unlike the others, Cockburn came to the methodology searching for efficiency rather than the need to constantly adjust to projects, which was an exciting distinction given his influence on the manifesto itself.

A few years later, in 1995, **Jeff Sutherland** and **Ken Schwaber** presented a solution to one of the biggest problems facing project management: customer-imposed systems. Often, customers would insist upon the organization putting specific metrics and methods in place to ensure delivery. However, the systems insisted upon were usually out of date or disruptive. This perplexed Schwaber, who took his question to a research team at DuPont—what was wrong with these methodologies at their core? After researching thoroughly, the DuPont team returned with a few critical points:

1. Organizations treated these imposed methodologies as well-understood processes when they were not actually properly thought out.
2. Organizations implemented methodologies without control; therefore, the processes were unpredictable.

Armed with this information and inspiration from the Japanese manufacturing industry, Schwaber and Sutherland worked on a new process to address these issues; they called it **Scrum**, after the rugby formation of the same name.

Almost in tandem with the development of Scrum, **Kent Beck** was developing his ideas for process development. In 1996, **Crystler** hired him to save the development of a payroll system. The project was a disaster; two months before delivery, there was little to no functional software. This resulted in a desperate Crystler CIO attempting to salvage the project, letting Beck begin from scratch with a smaller team. Exactly a year later, they had a live system with inexpensive maintenance and resalable. It was "a technical and business success," and it marked the first successful use of the **Extreme Programming (XP)** method.

These three distinct, yet similar solutions to the complicated issues present in the software industry were all decentralized, working independently of one another. Each had developed on its own, in a projected vacuum, yet rang with the same frequency. It was this realization that led to that industry-altering night in Utah—the unification of these ideas under one banner, in one document, would reshape the industry. The larger public could have adopted each of these ideas independently, but together, they could support broader themes. Agile became the definitive standard for software development. Apart from the most influential voices of the industry who expressed their support for the method, there are also five main reasons why Agile took off so successfully.

Benefits of Agile

The failures of the software crisis were numerous and often disastrous. The world Agile inherited was better, but project failure or ineffectiveness were still rampant throughout the industry. Those looking for a better way to provide value to complete software loads recognized five core benefits that attracted them to Agile:

1. The methodology produces a higher quality product.
2. Customer Satisfaction is baked in.

3. Realistic flexibility and increased project control are ensured.
4. The risk derived from systematic failure is reduced.
5. Faster ROI becomes possible.

A Higher Quality Product

Though the bar for this was low, Agile systems brokered significantly more successful projects and much less unused, wasted code. In 2013, researchers conducted a survey with project managers to understand the success rates of Agile projects v. Traditional projects. The results were:

Comparing IT project success rate by paradigm: 2013

Agile	Waterfall
○ 8% Failed	○ 18% Failed
○ 64% Succesfull	○ 49% Succesfull
○ 28% Challenged	○ 33% Challenged

Source: Clearcode S.A.: Agile v. WaterFall: Which Method is More Successful?

As expected, Agile projects develop a better quality product that is both less likely to fail or be contested by the customer after delivery. This leads to the second idea, as the customer ultimately defined the quality of the product, with whom the organization works closely.

Customer Satisfaction is Baked In

Agile principles and practices demand constant and consistent customer interaction and feedback. The customer satisfaction of any Agile project is of paramount importance; however, that is not the only reason why these projects succeed. Collaborative development does not only influence the final product itself, but also how the customer receives the product. If the customer can involve themselves to the point of also taking ownership of the project, beyond the successes of the development, they will feel unified by a desire to succeed.

This idea of "psychological ownership" stems from a 2006 study on physicians' acceptance of clinical information systems. In this study, researchers found that psychological ownership resulted in "user participation and crucial beliefs driving technology acceptance behaviors." They also found that the two most important factors in system acceptance were, unsurprisingly, the ease of use and perceived helpfulness.

When included in the development process, the customer can also define the usefulness of the project while also growing more familiar with its functionality.

Realistic Flexibility and Increased Project Control

For those working on the project, Agile is the pinnacle of control and flexibility through poignant dedication to communication and timeframes. Agile projects use sprints, shifting the team's direction and expectations of the project on the fly during or between iterations. The constant stream of communication that informs those shifts supports Agile project flexibility. For project managers and employees alike, the ability to adapt in accordance with the expectations of a client and the changing realities of a project makes all efforts more effective.

Reduced Risk Through Systematic Failure

Failing was not an option for traditional projects. There was a function meant to test the software within the WaterFall Method, but redeveloping an entire system after it had failed in the testing was exhausting and time-consuming. With the Agile methodology, errors are constantly laid out before the team as they are integrated in the system. Because the delivery of finished software is frequent, if it does not accomplish what it needs to or function as intended, the team can quickly reprocess it in a vacuum independently from the rest of the project. For traditional projects, failure meant the collapse of the whole project; however, in the Agile approach, you can perceive failure as an occasion for collective evolution.

The effect this has applies both to the team developing the system and the customer. Customers know they have time and opportunity to shift their expectations related to a project and trust the team to handle failure appropriately. Simultaneously, the project manager and group know they have the opportunity to adapt to changes or defeats. It's a win-win proposal.

Faster Return on Investment (ROI)

Because an organization can develop a product incrementally, a much faster delivery of market-ready products is also possible. After a few iterations, the team will have produced a functional product. This not only provides the company with a first-mover advantage, but it also contributes to the organization becoming more competitive thanks to the shortened delivery cycle. Furthermore, by allowing the client to define the essential features, the project team makes sure that they know exactly what is most important and most valuable for the client's business. Therefore, they can meet expectations and even exceed them early in the process, while delivering features in the most relevant order.

The benefits of Agile are as agile as the framework itself, affecting each team differently. The developers created the framework step by step, allowing it to develop along with the software industry. However, apart from the system requirements and customer satisfaction, Agile also provides a framework for a broader perspective toward product development in all fields. Agile, at its core, is the refinement of iteration ideals, customer integration, and focused functionality. We can apply these concepts to projects in every industry, not restricted to the software world. Agile has its roots in software design, yes. But it also learned from Japanese JIT manufacturing systems and principles of unit specialization. The functionality of a project is paramount in the Agile world.

Chapter Two Summary

- Agile is a collection of the best ideas in software development from 1965-2000.
- Those who influenced the Agile Manifesto maintain their own forms of Agile.
- The benefits of Agile projects extend not only to the team using it, but also to the customer receiving the final product.

The next chapter will explore components, ideas, and theories behind the Agile Project Lifecycle.

3

AGILE PROCESS

For all of its flexibility and independence, there is still a basic set of steps that teams using Agile methods need to take with each iteration. The **Agile Lifecycle** is a set of six steps that direct the workflow within a single iteration. The team would repeat this process over and over, focusing on individual pieces of a project in a continuous improvement cycle. But is a set system not entirely against the Agile principles of flexibility and development through customer demand?

Within every Agile project, there is an impulse to go toward one of two extremes: no planning or over-planning. It is difficult to foresee the final stages of the project, and given the aggressive reactionary nature of Agile projects, it can be tempting not to plan anything. This is a mistake. Agile projects often require more planning than their WaterFall counterparts for one reason: Agile acts as the management of information. To reiterate the past two chapters, we could describe Agile as adaptive, as it responds to the outside world. But it responds to carefully curated information. Forming systems helped by ideas like the Agile Lifecycle curate that information.

Over-Planning is also a net-negative. Over-planning can strain the independence of the team while putting pressure on them to predict an unpredictable future. There is a happy middle ground; rather than managing and planning for processes, the goal is to prepare the people involved in those processes. The Agile Lifecycle allows for that organization. There are six main phases of the Agile Lifecycle:

1. Planning
2. Analysis
3. Design
4. Coding
5. Testing
6. Development

Each of these serves a critical purpose in the development of the product while remaining authentically Agile. The Agile Lifecycle would not be project development system, but rather one specific idea: sprints.

Sprints are set periods given to an iterative development project in which the Agile Lifecycle occurs. They can vary in length, ranging from one day to 90 or more. Typically, a sprint will last 30 days; during that time, the team would complete a single life cycle and deliver the product to the customer. We are, of course, referring to feature-oriented projects that incrementally deliver a larger project. An important note: the Agile Lifecycle does not relate to the overall project life cycle—instead, it describes the more intimate sprints that collectively build up a larger project.

Stage 1: Planning

Planning is a significant failure point for many Agile projects in the beginning. As previously described, there is a constant temptation to swing toward one of the two planning extremes. An Agile project requires more preparation from a team; implementation of the team structure, communication, and other systems that enable flexibility are a critical part of this step. These planning phases, especially in an iterative process, are not about organizing the future. The Agile planning phase is a systematized search for value.

The goal of the planning process is not to establish rigidity; instead, it is to reduce risk and uncertainty, help with communication, and build trust within the team. For example, May 27 may be set as a feature delivery date in the planning process. However, as that date draws nearer, the team may need to postpone the delivery by a month in order to provide the quality required at the beginning of the project. This is acceptable, as the team should plan a buffer time for every project and remain flexible while also providing a certain level of predictability.

Risks cannot always be anticipated and avoided through planning with some kind of magical Agile technique. Instead, the company should focus on the very act of having a team go through the planning process itself, attempting to set dates, assume restrictions, and communicate about the overall goals. At its core, Agile planning is not about trying to develop a plan; in fact, it represents a system for planning. The difference lies in the output. While a WaterFall planning session might produce strict documentation that aligns with the customer's requirements, Agile planning sessions focus on current problems within the iteration and general expectations related to that feature, taking into account the current reality.

Agile planning typically involves more structure than WaterFall planning. Apart from establishing a base for communication and understanding of the specific iteration,

Agile is a chance to search for value. Stories, epics, and daily stand-ups support these searches, topics that we will discuss in full in chapter four. But because the planning stage consistently involves the customer in each iteration, the organization provides the team with the flexibility it needs to move forward.

There are two forms of Agile planning: **sprints** and **releases**. Planning for each requires a different involvement from the team and a certain shift in focus from the grander scheme to the detailed specifics of a single project. We will cover these more in depth in chapter four.

Stage 2: Analysis

Compared to typical project analysis, Agile again remains distinctly iterative and overall more feature-focused. The purpose of analysis within the Agile framework is to understand what the team will build, why they should do it, how long it will take, and in what order they should perform the various tasks. This applies to both the individual sprints and the larger releases. However, what the user searches for in a project will always determine the focus of these investigations.

Before delving into the analysis, we should note that there are a few things an Agile analysis is not. It is not an unnecessary step taken in the life cycle of a project, nor is it something that should be done for its own sake. From a development standpoint, it is a critical piece of the overall puzzle. Agile analysis accomplishes many things by focusing on a few core principles.

A focus on warm communication is critical within the analysis stage. Warm communication involves face-to-face interaction, video chats and combined team meetings, among other processes. Cold communication, comparatively, is highly documented and email-oriented. This stage should avoid that level of full documentation in favor of something that works as closely as possible with stakeholders.

This is a highly iterative process in the developing, building, and design processes, especially when attempting to predict delivery dates and overall project outcomes, the analysis process must be closely tied to the design process. One will naturally affect the other; therefore, it is best to develop the focus jointly. The analysis is also highly incremental, meaning that the project needs not rest on a single sprint. This allows the analysis to remain flexible within the parameters of the project.

The most important task that the Agile analysis fulfills, though, is twofold: it explores problems and develops timelines with a view to prioritizing projects. What the report results in is a set of estimations and evaluations for proposed sprints/releases. The main purpose of an analysis is to define the best strategy for the best customer ROI during the development phase. From this point, Agile analysis begins a game of prioritization led by the team. As a general rule, teams deliver the most critical features first. Not only does this allow buffer room for them to test and release the essential deliverables for the customer's convenience, but it also enables the customer to comment and adapt his or her expectations both earlier on the critical ideas and later on the less important features. The teams that can quantify, manage, and eliminate risk the fastest will find success. Agile analysis plays a major role in that search.

Finally, Agile analysis will develop a set of artifacts. These **artifacts** are systems, documents, templates, and spreadsheets that might be of use in future sprints or releases. In the name of efficiency, these are valuable assets to fall back on given the iterative process. They will allow the organization to process future sprints and releases faster, with the same consistency of the first sprints, by simply making a few alterations here and there.

Stage 3: Design

At this stage, the organization has made several decisions, determining the chronological order of the tasks and how to invest resources effectively. This portion of the life cycle explicitly addresses the technical questions of how the team should accomplish the task. Also known as **Software Architecture**, the process involves the team making high-level decisions regarding the overall design. The members of the group would have already asked many of the questions following the initial funding of the project. However, in this phase, they would specify and solidify the answers to these questions. In a traditional world, a business analyst creates the requirement model, which the architect who designs, models, then handles. Those models go to the coder, then to the tester, and so on. In an Agile design, developers work closely with stakeholders to better understand the latter's needs. The pair implements and tests solutions as they progress through the design process. It is not uncommon for the design to be closely linked to the functional coding portion—the separation is in that moment's focus outside of specific system changes.

The **test-driven development** (**TDD**) is a popular modern technique for the design process. This is an evolutionary approach to development where programmers write enough production code to pass a test. The primary goal of this activity is to allow programmers and teams to think the design through before writing functional code. Regardless of how one classifies the process, it works to answer the question, "Is the existing design the best possible to enable the functionality we need?" Because of the iterative nature of the Agile methodology, this question, in combination with the TDD process, allows for the delivery of practical frameworks for coding.

The negatives surrounding TDD strictly refer to the "minute mistakes" a programmer may make at a given moment. It is easy to create a functional code before the testing code, making the TDD an afterthought, and defeating the purpose. However, most of these concerns are addressed through systems like pair programming, where two programmers work side-by-side on one computer continuously. A true Agilist would refactor the application code or database scheme as they see fit to produce the best product possible.

Stage 4: Coding

The coding of a feature is the core work done in a project team. The focus of Agile coding does not lie on functional code; instead, everything comes down to a question of value delivery. In the manifesto and principles, the Agile Alliance explicitly spoke of a focus on "technical excellence." Not only programmers need to uphold this standard, but more so, the managers who allocate the resources to them.

Attention to technical excellence suggests that the completed code contains lines that the team can reasonably assess as free of defects. There is a minimization of technical debt carried over time, as the group builds quality and reliability into the software, and scalability is not an afterthought.

But this massive amount of effort is not just in the name of customer satisfaction. Though customer satisfaction is paramount (and stems directly from the functionality of the code), this focus on technical excellence also allows for a level of predictability. What technical excellence provides is a standard to refer to — it gives a clear and measurable way to define "done." Once a team works together for long enough, getting to "done" is much more predictable. But before they can wholly embed that experience of the community within the group, technical excellence becomes the standard. Not only do processes become more predictable, but the management is also provided with a verification mechanism and team members to complete the project.

Stage 5: Testing and Integration

The testing stage is a crucial split from the older, more traditional WaterFall methodologies. Rather than being sequential, Agile testing is a continuous process. Agile testing is a new age approach that focuses on testing in a smarter way instead of putting in extra effort and resources toward the end of a project. We can characterize this method by its distinction from typical WaterFall testing, which focused on a much more extensive test of the final delivery rather than the iterative testing seen here.

We apply Agile testing minimally. Rather than having a specific structure surrounding the trial, including dates and methods, we focus on the short-term delivery of short-term features. This, again, distinguishes the Agile approach from the WaterFall method, as the latter has lots of structure and focuses more on the production of a detailed description surrounding the final functionality of a product. While Agile testing is very well suited for smaller projects, Water-Fall testing has been adopted more often for larger projects.

This lesser specialization allows for Agile to remain nimble during the development of larger projects.

The smaller scale of Agile testing allows for a few improvements during the process. Because it shifts toward functionality, it involves less documentation. Instead, Agile testing focuses on delivering a product that will speak for itself. Furthermore, the iteration allows for testing during the creation of the product rather than following the completion of the development phase.

One of the most impressive aspects of Agile testing is the requirement for user acceptance at the end of each sprint. The negative is the pressure put on the customer for their involvement, but the benefits far outweigh the disadvantages. Not only can the product be adjusted during development, based on customer specifications, but the overall customer satisfaction can also grow with each user's acceptance. This acceptance, too, can be tracked and used as a KPI, allowing for iterations in the process before the start of a new sprint or release.

There are seven critical principles to a successful Agile testing phase. First, **testing is continuous**. This is the only way to ensure the ongoing progress of the product. This means that members of the team, individually or collectively need to test the functionality of the code. The continuous testing leads to the second principle: **continuous feedback**. It is through this concept that a product will not successfully meet business needs because there was a miscommunication somewhere within the process. Getting the feedback needed is a critical step of the testing phase. The team needs to ask the customer, "Is this what you wanted this feature to do?" If they reply enthusiastically, testing must still apply the third principle: **tests performed by the whole team**. In a traditional cycle, a specific test team conducts each test. In Agile, there are not only test teams, but also developers and business analysts who finalize and write off the product as passing their tests.

From here, the test observes the fourth principle: **decreased feedback time**. Because the team is involved throughout the process, their feedback should be immediate and thorough. The previously presented principles are only in place to enforce this single idea: the issues of the software must be communicated as quickly as possible. Decreasing feedback time is, therefore, the priority of any business team testing products in accordance with the Agile methodology. Once the feedback is provided, the programming team, under the guidance of the business, testing, and analysis team, addresses defects and cleans code *within the same sprint*, adhering to the principle of **simplified & clean code**. This enables cleaner code to pass to the development stage, making user acceptance more probable. Finally, the principles of **less documentation** and **test-driven implementation** round up the list by insisting upon functional code over a description of test results. The product is finally tested at the time of application—another contrast with the WaterFall method, in which testing would follow afterward.

Stage 6: Deployment

Though the organization completes testing and implements the software onto the system, the job is still not over. Deployment and maintenance of the final software product represent the end of a specific sprint or release. Also known as the "end game" or "transition," this phase contains five different aspects of testing and implementation that enable a successful deployment.

1. Final testing

This involves a testing of the last system with [AC1] acceptance testing. Though most of the trials should be completed during the construction phases (design, coding, testing), the final testing represents the last barrier that the code needs to pass to ensure compliance.

2. Rework

Inevitably, with Agile testing, issues and bugs will be uncovered. From there, the rework time is allotted for last-minute alterations before delivering the product to the client. The goal is not to address all defects that the team uncovers during the testing phase or introduce a second-stage coding phase; instead, the rework is meant for the significant, fixable bugs that may come up, with an emphasis on "good enough" over "perfect."

3. Finalization of any system and documentation

As free-flowing as Agile is with documentation, throughout the life cycle, there should be consistent documentation to present. The team would typically not finalize these until they complete the system release to avoid any extra work that might come up. Documentation, like all other requirements, needs to be cost-prioritized and created only as far as the stakeholders are willing to invest in it down the line. It is a waste of money to create mountains of documentation that nobody will read—supposing that the documentation requested is effective for the customer's needs. [AC1] In an iterative stage, this works to compare the accomplishments of the sprint to the larger goals established in the release; documentation therefore acts as a checklist that helps determine what the team has accomplished.

4. Training

This involves the customers' end-users, operations staff, and support staff in a deep learning environment on how to use the product effectively. Implementing training is customer-specific, though the Agile principles of communication apply here, too. This is a crucial component in the delivery of software, as it directly addresses the human element on the customer side. However, it is worth noting that the customer should be involved throughout to entire process.

5. Deployment of the system

This is a profoundly complex, critical aspect of Agile project management — the delivery. This is the moment that every preceding phase has been servicing. For this stage to be successful, the team needs to define a few vital pieces of information in advance:

- The deployment audience
- Understand precisely who the deployment will address and cater to the needs of the target audience.
- Deployment strategy
- Planning the communication, releasing meetings, and goals is just as essential as planning as the general architecture of the deployment. Release often, improving the deployment system throughout each iteration.

- Installation process
- This involves the testing of installation software and the creation of de-installation scripts.

Recognize that deployment is harder than it looks. It does not simply entail clicking upload and finishing, as many business executives assume. Well-tested software and consistently updated documentation make this phase easier. Ultimately, the team should determine and test this stage well before they reach it. Test, train, support, document, and deliver—once the software is deployed successfully, there is nothing left to do but to ensure the general maintenance of the program. Congratulations!

Chapter Three Summary

- The Agile lifecycle consists of six equally important stages.
- The stages insist upon constant communication, overlapping focuses, and general mindsets rather than specific rules and regulations.
- They are iterative; therefore, they are constantly improving based on previous versions of themselves throughout the product delivery process.

The following chapter will discuss the specifics of the planning phase, how that impacts the outcome of the project, and why Agile plans fail.

4

PLANNING FOR SUCCESS

The trapping modern mindset surrounding planning is specification production; planning is a function of the project it produces. Agile turns that premise on its head and asks a compelling question: "What if planning was the purpose?" The Agile argument is simple, especially in software development, as plans fail. They often fail and fail *hard*—it is a reality impossible to ignore. Therefore, the benefits of the plan do not lie within the final documentation itself, nor a specific outline of dates, costs, and ideals for solving problems that do not exist until halfway through the development process. Imagine there is a baby in the bathwater—rather than throwing out the entire bath, Agile focuses on nurturing the benefits of planning rather than wasting time and effort associated with a plan. It is a slight difference, but it shifts the focus of the project team dramatically.

One of the main reasons while Agile plans exist is to ensure the functionality of the project within other business units. This is vital for practicality, such as planning a marketing campaign, sales and customer training, release activities, and other aspects of business outside of the product design. Within the Agile team, however, the "plan" and the "planning" are two very different ideas.

Overall, the goal of Agile planning is to "iteratively arrive at an optimized answer to the ultimate new product development question of what should be built." Compare this to the focus of traditional, upfront planning. Using that system, teams attempt to construct scopes and schedules and allocate resources based on an existing set of parameters. This is great for traditional problems, like the construction of a physical building—there is an inspected, stable set of property, a limited amount of resources to use, a timeframe, and a completed expectation.

Software development differs from construction, though. The problem with building a new apartment complex is straightforward: "There is no apartment building here, and the customer wants an apartment building here." Compare this to an Agile project—the customer articulates a problem with a set of resources, then tells a story, or *epic*, concerning the issues they encounter and hope for the software to fix. The stories and expectations can flow and change throughout the development process. Furthermore, the solutions are not as straightforward as "construct an apartment building." While there is room for variability, we can approach Agile projects from infinite directions to accomplish a single task, taking into account variabilities in programmers, existing systems and infrastructure, and the overall goal of the larger project. It is because of this inherent variability that concrete plans fall apart for a software team, and why the development of a new form of planning was needed.

A critical feature of Agile planning is how we define the problems. Rather than placing the burden on the customer and asking them to define a solution for each specific iteration, the customer would simply explain a "story" to the development team. It is possible to convey the information within a narrative rather than specifics. Planning based on stories allows for general estimates relying on experience. Imagine going to a restaurant and asking for a large drink; is the specific number of ounces that important? Or are you drawing on a certain level of expertise to predict the size of this drink? When planning for a customer requirement, we can apply the same logic. You know how large the drinks are at other restaurants, acknowledge your level of thirst, and can subsequently attribute the expectations of this experience based on the size relative to those different experiences.

There is a functional system that enables this to occur —**story points**. These are relative units of measurement for the overall size of a particular feature. Once the customer conveys a complaint to the project team, the latter will assign a set of values to each element. A story that appointed a *three* was appointed to should be three times more complicated than a *one*; a *two*, twice; and so on. These numbers do not associate with the general difficulty, but also the size of the story. There is no set formula for determining the size of a story—a story point merely estimates the collective efforts that the team needs to put in to complete the entire feature in its complexity, to assess the risk attached to it, and any other aspects that they wish to include.

Two common ways to work with story points are rather intuitive. The first is to define the smallest story point as a *one*; from that point forward, use that story as the core unit to judge the rest. The second way consists of identifying a middle story and using it to establish a range. If the team wishes to use a 1-10 scale, this would be called the five-point story. Using that as an arbitrary base, the team then defines the rest of the stories based on the five.

The other critical metric to define before diving into the larger planning phase is the team's velocity. We can determine **velocity** (**V**) as the team's rate of progress—how fast they can complete story points (**P**) within one iteration. Similar to the story points, this is a metric relative to the project itself. However, it is also possible to estimate the velocity early on, bearing in mind the age and experience of a team. The team would calculate velocity by adding the total number of points accomplished within a standard sprint. For example, if in a two-week sprint the team completed a three-story with five, three, and six points, respectively, the team's velocity would equal 14.

The iterative nature of Agile project planning allows for the team to develop these metrics. Stories may re-appropriate points and initial velocities may change, but the functionality of the preparation is to improve predictions rather than rest on old data. This allows for a consistently updated set of times, ensuring that the customer is not caught off guard. If the total project is 50 points, and the first 2-week sprint resulted in ten points being delivered, it is safe to assume that the next 40 will take the relative time to complete, too. Based on these core metrics, Agile planning breaks up into three distinct horizons: the **Release**, the **Sprint**, and the **Day**.

This is the largest piece of planning an Agile team will typically do. Apart from representing an overview of a set of iterations, a **release** is also a connection to the larger project strategies and goals. Release planning works cyclically with the conditions of satisfaction to implement direction, scheduling, and budgets. Given these constraints, it moves to answer two questions: what do we want to solve, and how will that improve user experience? We accomplish this through a series of discussions surrounding eight key points:

1. **Needed features**: This portion of the discussion is for describing the targets of this specific release. The metrics of velocity and story points are not as prevalent in the discussion—consider this as the overview.

2. **Details**: At this stage, the discussion oscillates around the factors that can and will influence delivery. These include the required infrastructure, the risk associated with each goal, and any internal dependencies that may exist.

3. **Amount of work**: Quickly describe the amount of work needed for the release taking into account the goals established in the details.

4. **List of stories and epics**: Populate a list with the relevant stories and epics that you need to address by means of this release. From there, allocate story points.

5. **Adding iterations**: Develop a set of sprints that can address the story points within a

release. This includes questions of sprint length and lead times. It is best to keep iterations as short as possible, but typically this is not an option for early releases.

6. **Adding stories to iterations**: Slot times and sprints to address specific stories. Allocate the stories to each sprint based on risk and importance, in which you would approach the highest for each in easier sprints. If it is the first release, opt for general sprints instead of specifics in initiating the team and ideas.

7. **Adding more iterations**: Make sure you address all user stories for that release or remove lower-priority user stories and adapt the iteration framework accordingly.

8. **Communicate the plan**: Ask for feedback from the members of the team, product owner, and other stakeholders.

A release plan covers a significantly longer [AC1] period than a sprint plan—typically between two to six months. It is used to develop the planning of the first iteration and guide the others into a cohesive unit. As with most things Agile, you would update a good release plan during the execution of the projects, typically at the start of each iteration. This way, the plan will properly reflect current expectations about what you will ultimately deliver. Though releases may be variable in their lengths, they act as a final deliverable to the customer. Within this plan lies a long list of shorter, independent iterations, also known as sprints.

All sprints mostly follow the Agile life cycle independently. We perform **sprint planning** or *iteration planning* at the beginning of each iteration. Given the overall scope provided by the release and the focus of the recently accomplished sprint, the team identifies the next highest priority/risk work. The fact that this is a more micro-deliverable is reflected in the flexibility that accompanies its planning phase. However, a successful sprint planning also includes eight different points that help guarantee success.

1. **Retrospective meeting**: The goal of this meeting is primarily to learn from past sprints— what went well, which areas need improvement, and so on. It is a forum that enables the constant growth articulated in the Agile principles.

2. **Update sprints**: Plan pieces of the new sprint ahead of time, within the context of the larger release. Update the sprint based on the reality of the moment; shift priorities, anticipate new features, adjust for idle time, and so on—all of this with a view to avoiding surprises.

3. **Ensure detailed user stories**: The user story fuels the sprint—like a fire, the more fuel available to the team, the more the team has to go off of to produce a top-of-the-line product.

4. **Break stories into tasks**: Break the story's solution into digestible tasks. Sizable chunks like "Front-end for..." and "back-end for..." are desired, but the size of the tasks needs to remain small, requiring no longer than a workday.

5. **Assign tasks**: Distribute tasks based on each team member's commitment to performing them. In a Scrum framework, do this with a Scrum master. The team should contribute during the discussion portions based on skill sets.

6. **Physically write task**s: Create a communal, physical iteration tracker that extends and refers to the customer's story, the tasks assigned, and any other relevant information associated with the sprint.

7. **Track progress of tasks**: Add those responsible for the completion of each task to a grid, physical or digital record. Every job must have a responsible party attached to it. Included within this grid is the estimated time needed to complete the various tasks, remaining hours, and actual hours used. For the sake of transparent communication, this chart needs to be available to everyone on the team.

8. **Track velocity using burnout chart**: This chart should gather the data from the previous grid to determine an accurate team velocity. Chart the reality of the situation in tandem with the scheduled velocity. We should see any variability between the two plotted graphs as a sign that plans need to shift.

The Day

One hallmark of an Agile sprint is represented by the daily stand-ups. But beyond that, **daily planning** is a cornerstone of effective team communication. Agile takes this concept to the next level, enabling problem definition and solving to occur in a specific, daily forum. Furthermore, it works as a vehicle to connect relevant parties to problems and activities that the team needs to solve or redistribute. Have the entire team meet and report on their status each day, at a specific time. In an **Agile daily stand-up**, each team member efficiently addresses three main points:

1. What I did yesterday.
2. What I am doing today.
3. What is in my way?

These are as concise as they can be—a maximum of 15 minutes for the entire team. Usually, the team stands up to encourage that brevity (hence the term), so each member has no more than one minute to report. The status of a project or global effort can only be "Done" or "Not Done," with the numbers of hours left till completion if deemed "Not Done." State obstacles briefly to make the team aware of them, but also discuss them later in an appropriate forum. It is the responsibility of the manager to help the team overcome these obstacles by organizing the forums, asking the right questions, and providing the group with the resources needed to overcome the problems as quickly as possible.

The disparity between Agile planning and WaterFall planning is clear from the very beginning of the planning stages. In the traditional WaterFall sense, planning is attempted differently. Often, WaterFall planning comes across as very linear and activity-focused rather than value adding. Agile works to attack the eight critical failures of traditional planning systematically.

Planning as an activity rather than a feature

WaterFall methods of planning treat the process as something to service the other value-adding parts of the project rather than seeing it as an opportunity for profit enhancement. The customers themselves don't experience the benefit of an activity because it only facilitates the rest of the team's work.

Agile planning shifts this mindset to a service-oriented, solution-focused process, defined by problem-solving rather than mere organization. At the core of Agile planning is the customer story—based on this story, we develop the solutions and include them in a plan. Conversely, with WaterFall planning, the customer experience is one-dimensional.

Activities don't finish early

Parkinson's Law of 1957 is a reality that we must recognize when dealing with human nature. It is challenging to fight within an organization. A task will expand to take up the time allotted for its completion: no less. The programmer who allows seven days for a project will take seven days to finish it, even if they could have completed the work in a focused three days.

The law succinctly states a reality in its failure: activities are not finished early. Agile addresses this potential failure by setting a time limit within each iteration, thus enforcing constant production and turnover. However, traditional methodologies do not have this functionality in place and often plan ineffectively because of it; as a result, also produces a plan that is flawed and ineffective with the one resource it is attempting to manage: time.

If processes do not have an appropriate time designated to them, the only option available is to take the time or other resources from the following procedure. In a traditional model, there is a natural dependency between processes. Agile addresses this swiftly through independent iterations with their own personalized, evolutionary planning periods.

Furthermore, if a team requires multiple aspects for a project to complete it before they can begin, this produces a weak link situation. Let's say that moving on to testing requires the team to complete three tasks. Tasks one and two rest at 100% completed, but task three sits at 75%. An Agile process would never run into this issue because of the independence of each iteration. In a traditional method, though, the first two development teams must wait until the third can develop their product.

Multitasking cause further delays

A **1993 study by Clark and Wheelwright** articulated the effects of multitasking on productivity, finding an increase in productivity between the first and second tasks, but subsequent decreases from the third, fourth, and fifth tasks. When the team completes activities later than originally stipulated in the traditional planning scenario, the plan itself is not flexible enough for various tasks to be moved around. Therefore, the team must either move its break time by focusing production on the late deliverable or begin the new deliverable with the burden of the unfinished one. Both are bad options. Multitasking, though often the most seductive option, typically extends the completion date of work and leaves the work in progress much longer. It merely provides the illusion of speed.

Again, Agile methodology planning avoids this by orienting itself as a feature-focused and iterative process, demanding the total attention on a single production task each day. There are dangers related to multitasking, but they stem from the interconnectedness of the process rather than a rush caused by poor planning. The team elects the difference, **multitasking v. necessity-based multi-tasking**—one being inherently more manageable than the other.

Features are not developed by priority

Traditional methodology planning is not for the customer. More than anything, traditional WaterFall methodology focuses on satisfying the existing organizational requirements of the development company and their executives.

Ignoring uncertainty

The Achilles' Heel of traditional planning is the ignorance of uncertainty. Again, the more straightforward processes, such as construction, minimize uncertainties. However, software development involves *massive* risks. Because of the rigidity of a traditional plan with the amount of organizational value placed on the development of the project early on, the WaterFall methodology inevitably misses an important future variable.

Agile avoids this by remaining flexible; depending on the size of the project, the following iterations can quickly absorb any uncertainties. From there, the team makes adjustments as needed, and shifts priorities based on the existing and future realities rather than an assumed ideal. This is one of the most significant benefits of Agile planning and organization over traditional rigidity.

Estimates become commitments

The more extensive plans produced in the traditional methods are automatically reported to higher executives and the customer as due dates. To reiterate, the nature of conventional methods focuses less on the product and customer and more on satisfying existing business frameworks. What results from this reality is the potential for commitment, hence more rigidity in the system. Suppose a project has a 0% chance of being finished within a week. An organization can guarantee to complete that same project by the 5-year mark. Every day in between has a percentage associated with the probability that the group will finish the work. If a team commits to a date, the chance that they will not complete the project by that point increases. Therefore, the commitment to any practical time comes with the risk of the task not being completed.

Both traditional and Agile recognize this as a problem and address it accordingly. However, the difference lies in how Agile accomplishes this systematically through its iterative process. Traditional methodology merely encourages in-depth estimations associated with delivery dates.

The function of planning is critical to the development of a final product. It serves as an opportunity to add value to the final product, involve the customer, and explore new solutions for emerging problems. Agile planning runs based on a few assumptions, but all of them are customer-oriented and organized to deliver the best product.

- Planning is a value-enhancing stage for both the customer and the development team.
- Agile planning is designed to operate within the blind spots of traditional planning.
- Moving from traditional to Agile is a shift in mindset as much as it is a shift in organizational systems.

The next chapter will be exploring the differences in communication styles between traditional methods and Agile ones.

5

AGILE COMMUNICATION

Many factors can define success because success is different depending on the individual, the metrics and the tools needed. For someone like Tiger Woods, success may be winning the Masters golf tournament, but he can determine the metrics and tools he uses to do that based on earlier, smaller successes such as hitting an extra yard at the range. Compare this to ideas of a figure like Warren Buffett, who defines the most significant measure of success to be "people [thinking] well of you" rather than the size of a bank account, or a parent who sees success within their child's progress. Agile contains diversity at an individual level because a long list of different metrics and tools is used to develop into that larger triumphant moment.

Agile projects do not individually define the metric. Instead, they define **success** as the delivery of a beyond satisfactory project to the customer. Metrics will ebb and flow based on the customer and situation, as in the design of the Agile methodology. However, there is an underlying critical metric that consistently leads to the success of an Agile project: communication.

Miscommunication, under-communication, or poor

communication of any type in an Agile project unequivocally leads to the collapse and failure of said project. The philosophies behind Agile communication do not express the threat of failure, but rather the benefits of increased and transparent communication. Agile exists in a world where failure to communicate is all too easy, though. The purchasing department often exports "good communication" after insistence upon the use of a technological system. By comparison, developing an organizational, project-, and team-specific communication system takes much less time and can feel more productive.

The stakes are too high within an Agile project. Exporting the role of communication may work for a traditional WaterFall system, but the core functionality of an Agile team relies on and beyond their ability to communicate effectively and efficiently. An Agile team must also be able to react to miscommunication. Catching miscommunication quickly enough means ensuring the success of the project: failure begets failure.

But there is hope! This chapter will look into the many differences between traditional and Agile communication, the specific value-enhancing opportunities within Agile communication, tactics used within the Agile community, and values that lead to sound systems.

The Core of Agile Communication

Before analyzing the specifics of these systems, let's investigate project management communication. There are core values of project management communication that pave the way to success, despite the status or particular methodology. However, the main functionality of conversation in a project team is derived from trust.

If a development team is consistently misappropriating

time to coding tasks, a manager has two options: he or she can trust the metrics put forward by the team, which suggest the project will take two weeks, or they can trust the developer, who is arguing for. Which alternative should the manager choose?

Regardless of the final decision, the development team must receive feedback. Should the manager go with the metrics, the development group might conclude that they can ask for even more time in the next iteration. However, should the manager go with the development team's suggestion, this may affect the product delivery date. The cycle will repeat over and over again.

A lack of trust is not an issue only in the software world. In inventory management, we describe this lack of confidence as "**The Bullwhip Effect**." Poor communication, shifting expectations, and a lack of trust in a system cause adjustment to be made around individuals rather than realities. It creates a reaction reinforced by another, which spirals into a new reality altogether. Regardless of the system, the key to effective communication is *trust*: one individual must have faith that another's words are valid.

In traditional software development methodologies, companies typically facilitate this through documentation. The organization solidifies communication with the customer in a contract and the system requirements at the beginning of a development project. From there, they hand the project down from team to team, each trusting that the initial conditions still satisfy the customer's needs. They are passing down a trusted reality from one unit to another. Accomplishing these tasks as a team will lead to success.

Agile communication involves very little documentation. In addition, the expectations expressed at the beginning of a project are, by design, constantly changing throughout the implementation, iterations, and overall conversations with the customer or end-user. Because of this disparity between the consistency of a traditional project and the teetering chaos of an Agile one, trust is of the utmost importance. Teams need to systematically develop confidence in Agile projects, for an *assumption* of faith may lead to problems reminiscent of the bullwhip effect.

More than preventing failure, Agile communication adds value. The constant feedback loop with the customer, the fluidity between teams, and the rapid problem definition lead to a more satisfied customer. Teams cannot accomplish any of these if they undermine trust. With that focus, what are the systematic changes that we can make to a traditional model to make it Agile?

Traditional v. Agile Approaches to Communication

As discussed, much of the traditional model relies heavily on the foundation of documentation. But beyond the base of documentation, there are many systems, tools, and tones within traditional communication that differ from the Agile counterparts. In the following principles, we highlight many of these differences:

---

4. Business people and developers must work together daily throughout projects.

6. The most efficient and effective method of conveying information to and within a development team is face-to-face conversation.

7. Working software is the primary measure of progress.

10. Simplicity - the art of maximizing the amount of work not done - is essential.

12. At regular intervals, the team reflects on how to become more effective, then tunes and adjusts its behavior accordingly.

Traditional communication has the luxury of being an afterthought, a tool to clarify the existing structure provided by general documentation. Agile does not have that structure. Therefore, its approaches must be different.

Face-to-Face Communication

One of the main differences in Agile communication practices is the emphasis on a communication hierarchy: not all forms of communication are not equal. We describe this in the sixth Agile principle, which states that the "most efficient and effective method" of communication is **face-to-face contact**. **Alistair Cockburn** pushed and expanded this idea in 2002 with this graph:

Copyright 2002-2005 Scott W. Ambler
Original Diagram Copyright 2002 Alistair Cockburn

Though the times and technology have transformed since Cockburn developed the theory, the hierarchy remains. As teams and companies become more and more remote, challenges of communication have remained a consistent issue. The tools may have changed and evolved, but the paradigm is still relevant to this day. Though Cockburn felt strongly about the **Plain Old Whiteboard** (**POW**), the lesson he wished to convey was not only one of complete superiority.

Despite delivering the most information in the most effective manner, face-to-face meetings are not always preferable to documentation. The key to face-to-face communication is nuanced—understand when it is superior to other methods. With a remote team, would a face-to-face conversation be practical? Not in the slightest. However, is a video call more valuable than a phone call? Bearing in mind the lessons of the sixth Agile principle, yes, a video call is preferable to a phone conversation. So, when is documentation preferred?

Documentation v. Gathering of Artifacts

With such a high trust factor enabling the entire communication aspect of traditional project management, documentation is scrupulous and complex. The process typically bookends the development, starting with the initial requirements and comparing them with the final delivery. During the development phase, documents comprise progress and comprehensive status reports, as well as the less formal communication over email and other platforms. The phase can be process-driven, which allows a structure of reliance to develop. While this may work for some projects, an Agile-oriented project must abandon this reliance. What replaces it is a more versatile approach to documentation.

The first shift, as with many pieces of Agile, is the change in mindset. An Agile approach views documentation as a value-enhancer, not as something transitive among value-adding efforts. Documents are not temporary, single-use items; they are artifacts transferred between teams, reused over multiple iterations, and changed or developed for the specifications of a single project.

We characterize artifacts by their intentional simplicity, providing information considered barely sufficient. This is a massive departure from the complex, dense documentation of traditional methods for one reason: sometimes, documentation is the best method of communication. However, when put in a head-to-head fight with other forms, the formalities and structure of documentation can weigh down, making it impractical. Agile removes these formalities and arrangements, opting for easy-to-deliver documentation.

Furthermore, the simplistic nature of the documentation impairs the ability of a team to revert to the traditional reliance upon it. The push toward a "show, don't tell" form of communication allows the team to record the most critical and relevant information while leaving the nuances of a project to the eyes of each questioner. Project teams use the "show, don't tell" concept throughout the execution of a project by showing working software in order to communicate progress and functionality. The regularity with which this transpires replaces the necessity for in-depth documentation. Compared to the burden of traditional documentation, Agile documentation functions well within the iterative and demanding framework of a project team.

Meetings

In the U.S. alone, 55 million meetings happen every day. The traditional business meeting may have a few negative characteristics. Meetings themselves "suffer" from the previously mentioned Parkinson's Law and, therefore, are typically longer than they need to be. Another common complaint is related to the people present in any meeting— many end up attending meetings where they are not actually needed. Finally, there is often a failure to define the success of a session. These flaws of the meeting culture run rampant in traditional style settings. So, when establishing a new set of rules for meetings, the Agile Alliance attempted to address these flaws with a new system.

The first issue was winning the impossible fight with Parkinson's Law. The law states that "work expands so as to fill the time available for its completion." Meetings often take one hour when, if no one designates a length of time for the meeting, the team cannot complete the work and conversation in 15 minutes. Agile meetings address that idea specifically by setting a goal: be as quick as possible. Strip down everything else; how long should this meeting take? This approach is best seen in the daily stand-up, a maximum 15-minute session in which participants answer three predetermined questions as concisely as possible. The underlying assumption is this: more time in a meeting does not equal more information, nor does it equal more value. Therefore, don't waste this valuable resource of a team. Keep the meeting concise and win the war against Parkinson's Law.

The second fight is with the all too common issue of having people in a meeting who should not even be there. Only the most relevant parties, who stand to benefit from the meeting, should be included in the attendance list. The daily stand-up need not involve the customer, lest it is of immediate benefit to them and the rest of the people in the conference. The invitation or attendance list of a meeting gives certain clues as to the relevance of the information that individual can present and his or her expertise in relation to the problem discussed. The benefit of face-to-face communication lies in the significance of the parties present —Agile communication relies on the wisdom of the manager to call meetings with intentionality and efficiency. After all, the structure of an Agile meeting is to provide enhanced productivity to the collective team, not reduce it.

Chapter Five Summary

- Agile communication is built on trust, which in turn is formed with the help of documentation.
- Artifacts replace complex documentation.
- Consistent, short meetings replace longer, drawn out meetings.

The next chapter will dive into the specifics surrounding to common Agile method known as Scrum.

6

SCRUM BASICS

As described in chapter two, three central systems contributed to the foundation of the Agile Manifesto: Extreme Programming (XP), Crystal, and Scrum. Each of their respective founders has its name on the Agile Manifesto and exerts a significant influence over its principles. However, there is variety within the specifics of the systems following the establishment of Agile principles.

What **Ken Schwaber** and **Jeff Sutherland,** the founders of Scrum, built appears simple on the outside. From the inside, though, it is a notoriously difficult system to master and apply in even the most direct project. It isn't hard because of the activities that it requires a team to do. Instead, the difficulties of Scrum fall derive from what a team *cannot* do. Such teams cannot rely on Gantt charts or time reporting, nor can they rely on hierarchies and assigned tasks handed down from above. But nothing worth doing is ever easy, right? When applied correctly, Scrum principles and practices have achieved what many believed would be "impossible."

This chapter will serve as an overview of the world of Scrum—the rules and principles that lie at its foundation, an introduction to the terminology and roles within Scrum teams, and a quick look at the modern use of Scrum.

Scrum Essentials

The first thing to acknowledge is also the easiest: Scrum is Agile. It rests on all the Agile principles and ideals, which are customer centricity and involvement, face-to-face over documentation, value, and activities of transitive ones. Philosophically, Scrum and Agile will always empower a development team to satisfy the customer. Where Scrum takes a step forward is into the specifics surrounding the implementation of those values. More specifically, it entails a more creative development process based on the **Scrum Skeleton**:

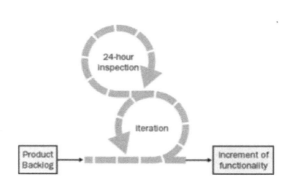

THERE ARE two things worth noting in this context: the vocabulary and the time scale. A product backlog is an ever-growing list of tasks that the team needs to complete. Increment of Functionality is *any* unit of functionality added toward the overall goal of the project. The way a Scrum team goes from backlog to functionality is through an iteration. Sound familiar? However, there is the added aspect of a time scale—a 24-hour daily inspection on the progress of an iteration. Think of this 24-hour inspection as a GPS continually updating the position of a project to make sure it is on the right path, also taking into account any new, emerging obstacles. Each time a team runs into new complexities or difficulties, the daily review of the iteration provides a system to identify the obstacles. From there, the team can decisively move forward with the best way to handle the issues. The team ultimately determines the success of the creative projects and acts as the heart of Scrum productivity. There is one more question that needs answering, though: Who *is* the team?

A **Scrum team** only consists of three roles: the product owner, the team, and the Scrum Master. Only people who have committed to the project can fill these roles; commitment means having something to lose if the project fails. the Scrum Master [AC1] designs these roles around responsibilities to others.

The **product owner** is responsible for the interests of everyone with a stake in the project and the resulting system(s). The owners create the funding, return on investment objectives, release plans, and look at the overall requirements. They do this through the backlog, making sure that the team first addresses the components with the highest functionality and importance in the earliest iterations, then builds upon them.

The **team** converts a backlog order to product functionality. We cannot define a Scrum team —there are no existing hierarchies, as it is a group of individuals who possess different skills. Teams are self-managing, self-organizing, and cross-functional. It is their job to figure out how to convert within a single iteration. Because of this high level of responsibility, team members are collectively responsible for the success or failure of each iteration and the project as a whole.

Finally, we have the **Scrum Master**. The Scrum Master is the *Scrum referee*. Their job is to teach Scrum principles, implement Scrum to function within the context of a company's culture, organize the Scrum process, and ensure that everyone follows the Scrum principles. The following sections outline the Scrum principles that the Scrum Master enforces.

The 6 Scrum Principles

Scrum conforms to Agile principles, but it also proposes six new principles that fall within Agile frameworks. These work specifically in Scrum teams and should not be applied to other Agile projects indiscriminately.

1. Empirical Process Control

Three core ideas motivate Scrum and allow it to function as exceptionally as it does: transparency, inspection, and adaptation. The three function in tandem with one another, shifting as the core functionalities of process control. This is a constant, verifiable system balanced by each of the functionalities.

2. Self-Organization

A modern worker with unlimited access to information, tools, and training can deliver significantly more value if he or she is self-organized. This does not only result in better team buy-in through a sense of shared ownership, but it also fosters an environment of creativity and innovation that goes beyond what is possible in a restrictive hierarchy.

3. Collaboration

There are three core aspects to this principle as well: awareness, articulation, and appropriation. Once a group can self-organize, the members must collaborate and use each other's strengths appropriately. They only achieve this through communication and interaction—based on these values, a more significant sum than that of the parts emerges.

4. Value-Based Prioritization

This principle specifies the value as the metric with which to evaluate success and scheduling. The goal of any Scrum is to deliver maximum business value as early as possible.

5. Time-Boxing

In Scrum, teams consider time as the limiting constraint. This idea is used to help manage projects based on an organization of time over other limiting resources (funding, contact, etc.). The fundamental assumption is that time will limit Scrum; therefore, it must be organized and properly used by the team.

6. Iterative Development

This principle works to reinforce the Agile principles of iteration while also distributing the product owner/customer and the organization's responsibilities. Repetition is the primary mechanism for product development—more specifically, the product needs to adapt and improve continually.

As with many forms of Agile product development, we can use the principles of Scrum outside of the software development world, too. Any industry or project that is highly variable, produces functionality over time, and suffers from hierarchies and dependencies can use Agile principles. One of the best fields for this approach is modern marketing and social media. Let's look at how companies can apply Scrum principles to something other than software development.

A traditional marketing team runs similarly to a conventional software team. There is a massive amount of development and documentation upfront, the process typically leaves out the end-users beyond the few inputs that bookend the project, and the overall experience of the project hinges largely on a hierarchical team delivering a final, massive product. But as times have changed, so has the marketing world. How have these two unsuspecting cousins evolved since the days of madmen on Saks Fifth? Viewed through the eyes of Scrum principles, there are three key areas that have changed: **customer interaction**, **team structure**, and **tactical evolution**.

Customer Interactions

Social media and the Internet have completely changed marketing landscapes. The past forms of coupon-based customer engagement have their limitations. Nowadays, the world contains real estate for everyone in the style of public social media profiles.

Scrum and Agile principles define the end-user as the core customer, while also demanding intimate and personal communications over essential documentation. Technology has enabled these ideas to be a reality on a mass scale.

Beyond the rapid evolution of AI systems like Chatbots or Search Engine Optimization systems, it is possible to contact active customers directly, on a multitude of forums. The interaction does not define success in these forums, however.

Once again, Scrum and Agile principles define success by the consistent deployment of working, finished software, emphasizing solution-based achievements rather than metric-oriented ones. In marketing, it is the customer who determines if a solution can solve the problem to begin with, never mind the functionality. From a social media perspective, this shifts the focus from the ever-tempting trap of chasing likes to chasing legitimate, intimate customer interactions and engagement. A solution may answer a customer's question as much as it may engage with them physically, where they believe they need physical interaction. For example, look at Dirty Lemon's pop-up store in the middle of New York City. Customer interaction is the foundation of modern marketing, as it always should have been. But somewhere along the way, marketing organizations get caught up in corporate hierarchies and bureaucracy that come with a big budget. How can Scrum and Agile principles combat those issues?

The Scrum Team

One of the most significant points emphasized in a Scrum team is the independence given to each member. A truly Scrum-organized team has lots of motivation and self-organizes. Furthermore, the only people allowed on a Scrum team are those with a legitimate stake in the outcome of a project.

The principal factor of the social media team's success lies in its autonomy to represent the entire brand. To do this effectively, the team must be in constant, effective communication with the various business departments. If there is an issue with the product, the customer needs to inform the team so they can field questions. Is the sales team independently engaging customers via social media? Modern teams remain informed. Because of the constant shifts and changes in customer expectations, with clients wishing for example, that a brand's Twitter account is both entertaining and informative, teams must put in place certain communication systems that support this highly iterative demand.

Even so, the systems mean nothing if the hierarchy is present. While guidelines and expectations are legitimate, the highly iterative function of the organization is only productive if they can deliver the functionality intact. A social media team cannot be engaging if interactions must first pass through a larger hierarchy—the timeline is too short. If a marketing executive must approve every action, nothing will get done. On the other end, Scrum plans last into infinity; the members must be able to pace and control their production. The second critical aspect, as defined by Scrum and Agile, is the empowerment of the team to deliver results. Trusting the team to understand the situation and decide the best path forward is part of the Agile approach. The risks associated with this methodology derive from how the entire trust in a brand is placed in the hands of one employee sitting behind a computer, where one tweet could undermine or destroy years of work. And the upside?

Adaptive Efforts

The most considerable upside to Agile and Scrum planning is how they force teams, by design, to adapt continually. By shifting focus to the end-user, a social media team will encounter constant shifts and changes. This can manifest in different platform engagements, daily news cycles, or shifting customer preferences. But if a social media team is running a Scrum-esque system of constant verification and improvement, this is no problem. It is expected and planned for within the systems that support their efforts.

Scrum teams welcome shifts as opportunities to offer value to customers. They focus on simplicity over intricate design, because they don't have time for overwhelming complexity — they need to deliver, now and in the next moment. Scrum teams have 24-hour review systems in place to catch changes in a trend and adopt it to the present reality; in addition, they subscribe to the notion that yesterday's plan is today's failure. While that doesn't have to apply to constructions, in the meticulous and convulsing world of social media, the last twelve hours barely apply to current plans anymore.

Scrum teams adapt. Moreover, they adjust depending on the goals and defined successes of the systems in which they operate. Scrum teams have the power to make those changes without the burden of traditional hierarchies. But most of all, they deliver constant and simple solution-based products to the end-user. The principles of Scrum and Agile go beyond the software development world—both principles bleed into any reality dependent on the shifts of that reality over the constants that build it. The set of tools used to manufacture this reality comes down to a set of specific Scrum meetings.

Types of Scrum Meetings

Unnecessary meetings are the death of a Scrum team's effectiveness, and organizations should avoid them like a fourteenth-century plague. Based on this loose principle, there is a specific design to productive Scrum meetings that goes beyond a simple agenda and an efficient note-taker. Though release do meetings exist, we will not discuss them in this chapter, as the Agile team does not get involved as profoundly.

Sprint Planning

The stated existence of a sprint planning meeting is rather straightforward—determine the goals of the next iteration. Scrum dives into the weeds with keys to a successful meeting, but we will discuss that later in the chapter. As an overview, sprint planning meetings comprise two four-hour parts: prioritization of the backlog and organization of the sprint.

The product owner of the team conducts and organizes the prioritization of the backlog. During this portion of the meeting, they will present the purpose, meaning, and intentions of this backlog organization. Within that timeframe, the product owner should articulate all crucial aspects and details that can ensure the earliest shipping time. At the end of the four-hour meeting, once the team knows enough, they should select as much as they believe they can deliver as a potentially functional product by the end of the sprint. Typically, a lunch break follows.

The product owner does not spend the four hours following the lunch break asleep at the desk—instead, they hand the reins to the team to lead the session. Because the teams are self-organizing and responsible for the final deliveries, they develop their tentative sprint plan. More tasks will emerge as the sprint proceeds and planning meets the contact of the enemy, but a tentative sprint plan allows the ball to roll in the best direction. The 30-day sprint timebox brings the end of the second four-hour meeting; the time is on!

Daily Scrum

The **daily scrum** is a slightly altered version of a *daily stand-up* meeting. The basic questions associated with a stand-up expand upon three specific tools for facilitating the meeting:

1. "What did you do on the project since the last daily scrum meeting?"
2. "What do you plan on doing on this project between now and the next daily scrum meeting?"
3. "What impediments stand in your way between meeting your commitments to this sprint and this project?"

The purpose of the meeting also remains consistent, with a focus on synchronizing of the team toward a collective effort; however, the daily scrum is somewhat different because of the independence offered to the team. This self-organization allows for flexibility within the group, which means that energy can be distributed cross-functionally and internally rather than solely relying on external help.

Sprint Review

Teams would hold this meeting at the end of a sprint as another four-hour time-boxed meeting. In this meeting, the group presents what they have developed. This way, they illustrate functionality and determine the next steps of the organization.

Sprint Retrospective

After the sprint review, but before the next planning meeting, the Scrum Master holds a three-hour sprint retrospective. The goal of this meeting is to provide a forum for system improvement, reflect on lessons learned during the sprint, review the applied Scrum principles, and ensure an improved development process for the next sprint. Apart from questions of effectiveness, another important aim of this meeting is to ensure that the team enjoys the process. The design ensures the longevity of the team's efforts, but more practically, it provides feedback on the social relationships present in the team and enables strength through unity.

Keys to a Successful Sprint Meeting

The motivations and mindsets behind a successful Scrum sprint meeting are distinct from traditional planning meetings. Especially if a group is shifting from the classic framework to a Scrum setting, the sprint meeting is the first test of reimagined roles, self-organization, and authority of new parties. But there are also very human interactions, the nuances of which need to be respected, especially given the reliance upon a self-determined team.

As a general framework, the first mindset to address is that of the Scrum Master. Often, when putting together a Scrum team, the Scrum Master is a former boss or manager. This can work if one difficult condition is fulfilled: the former boss must shift from manager to coach. It is difficult to shake management habits after years of application, as even the smallest seeping through old techniques can corrupt the new team altogether. While it may be more efficient, the team will lose the real power of Scrum. This undermining of self-organization can come up in other aspects of the process.

A team needs to feel physically supported. This seems like a little thing, but it is actually critical to the team's development and functionality in its quest for self-organization. It is the little things that support this notion rather than large gestures. Does the idea of twelve people standing around a whiteboard with one marker in a room made for four scream "power" through self-organization? Not at all, and that sensation is experienced by the team. The quickest and most effective way to make the team feel empowered is to shower them with support from the beginning. Make sure there is a big enough room for the team there and provide them with materials like pens, paper, sticky notes, whiteboards, and markers. Invest in some healthy snacks. Understand that, especially with a new team, it is important to convince them of their authority and a sense of support—it is the little things that do that. Given how the first challenge a team will face is the sprint meeting, here are three critical areas that management can address to guarantee success.

Meeting Arrangements

Leave most meetings to the Scrum Master. It is their job to find the right people and determine the best ways to involve them. If the team is locally based, it is vital to have all members in one room. If members are working remotely, it is critical to have them as close to face-to-face as possible. This means no microphone-muted phone calls while the employee does something else. Instead, it means an organized video call on Skype or another service with the remotely located employees being "projected" into the room. If little mobile iPad robots are available, use those—

anything to make the person feel as if he or she were in the room.

The Scrum Master also prepares and publishes the agenda. Typically, the number of weeks within a sprint (two hours for every one week, with eight hours as the maximum) determines the length of the meeting. A meeting beyond eight hours (four weeks) is no longer a Scrum sprint. Again, during the conference itself, support the team with materials, coffee, and some snacks.

Sizing Stories

Story points are one of the most critical tools used in a sprint meeting. After the product owner presents the stories, a team must have a reliable method of collectively attributing difficulty. Even if the metric used is the infamous story point, there are different methods to get to those values.

Poker planning, or **Scrumpoker**, was one of the earliest forms of point assignment. As explained by Scrumpoker Online, "The key here is discretion. Scrum poker or planning poker is a consensus-based, gamified technique to estimate the complexity and effort needed for the development of a software feature. After presenting the feature, each member of the team picks a vote from different ranges of card sets. The vote remains hidden until all members have voted in order to avoid influence from other team members. After everyone has voted, the people who have made the highest and lowest estimates explain their choice, and the process is repeated until the team agrees on a value." Cards might range from 1 to 40 points, and online options exist for remote teams as well!

Another standard option is the T-shirt method. Inexperienced Scrum teams would typically use this method. It adheres to the same ideas as Scrumpoker but uses something detached from a numerical base. For example, extra small (XS) might be worth 1 story point, while triple extra-large (XXXL) may be equivalent to 40 points. For the new teams that might not have a stance on velocity yet, it is always safe to use an eight-point starting velocity. The members of the team can adjust it throughout the first few sprints as they calibrate.

Scheduling

Beginning an iteration in the middle of the week results in an interesting mental shift for the team, as the relaxed slump of Friday work shifts to the effort driven by mid-iteration development. This single shift makes teams significantly more effective and is encouraging for any up-and-coming Scrum team. Apart from the team's boost in energy, there is also a second reason to begin mid-week.

Start Sprints mid-week

Beginning an iteration in the middle of the week has an interesting mental shift for the team, as the relaxed slump of Friday work shifts to the effort driven by mid-iteration development. This single shift makes teams significantly more effective and is an encouraging shift to any up-and-coming Scrum team. Beyond the team's boost in energy, there is a second reason to begin mid-week.

Never end with development on a Friday

You cannot rush the final development and implementation; you must monitor it. A load left to its own devices over the weekend has a chance of going wrong. With nobody there to watch the system, you can lose and damage work.

Respect employee time off

When scheduling, consider employee holidays, requested time off, and other long weekends. Understand how that will shift the realities of a sprint and plan accordingly.

Chapter Six Summary

- Scrum is a trust-based approach to complexity.
- A Scrum master is a coach, not a manager.
- Scrum principles can apply to any iterative project.
- The minutiae of a meeting matter.

The following chapter will discuss the intricacies of a second Agile methodology known as Kanban.

INTRODUCTION TO KANBAN

Scrum is a focused Agile system based on the idea that time is the limiting factor in a project. If a team can optimize time, then it will successfully deliver the project. It does this through strict timeboxes, drafting schedules around team-generated predictions, and prioritizes customer input and stories.

Kanban is another Agile system that takes a different direction when it comes to problem definition. While Scrum focuses on the limitations of time, Kanban shifts toward production as the limiting factor and views time as something the team can optimize, not a limitation. It still has a significant amount of customer input, remains Agile, and typically delivers excellent projects ahead of schedule. However, this one fundamental shift changes much about the dynamics, delivery, and process behind the system. Let's dive into the principles of Kanban to understand the difference between the two.

One massive difference between the two systems is immediately apparent in the way the teams organize. While Scrum defines three distinct roles, Kanban has none. It may involve a project manager or an Agile advisor at some point, but there are no expectations or requirements for those roles to exist. In Scrum, those jobs absorb into the team, including the organizational roles played by Scrum Master and project owner. How is work prioritized?

The Kanban System

Kanban focuses on a systematic, continuous flow of work. All efforts go through the **Kanban Board**, the importance of which cannot be underestimated. It is the game-changer that allows for Kanban to function. And in a traditionally Agile sense of humor, it is scarily simple. The board comprises three pieces: **Board, List**, and **Card**. It encapsulates the project or workflow, representing the entire workspace. On the board, there is a set of **three to six Lists**, depending on team process and preference. Each List is a space for related cards sorted by the name of the list, the latter of which we can name, "In Progress," "Done," "To-Do," "In Development," and so on. These lists are pieces of the process as divided by the team. Finally, there are the Cards. Cards contain a specific task that the organization has to complete. They connect the entire system, moving between boards and lists as the team works through the process in reality. Nothing about this fancy to-do list seems too impressive, but these elements come with a few rules that serve as the foundation of Kanban.

Kanban operates on a **pull system** of task processing. When tasks are "pulled," it means a specific team member has taken them over. This team member cannot take another card until they have moved the job to the "Done" List. Not only does this work prevent wasted time waiting on another person to finish their task, but it also works to avoid over-processing and rushed projects. This single run enables a continuous flow of effort not seen in other Agile practices.

The second rule is just as critical: each List has a limit to the number of cards. This allows a team to keep the flow to a smooth level by restricting the efforts aimed at specific sections of production. If one process comprises too many tasks, that means another piece is lacking attention. From there, an organization can shift focus, efforts, and people as needed. This helps with the battle against idle time and forces adaptability within the context of a team.

The approach is helpful when multiple projects with various sizing and priorities are running simultaneously. Furthermore, Kanban allows and encourages changes to the board within the process. The focus on workload optimization continues with how the organization can measure success.

While Scrum batch pulls an entire iteration's worth of projects, Kanban pulls whenever a team member finishes and is ready for more work. It is a shift from iterative delivery to continuous delivery and development based on the demands of the business. The focus of this application of Agile principles is on decreasing one metric: cycle time.

We measure **cycle time** by how long an entire project takes to complete; not a fraction nor a single iteration, but the whole project. While velocity and the Burndown chart in Scrum measure how efficient a team is working, Kanban uses the **Cumulative Flow Diagram** (**CFD**). This diagram visualizes how tasks mount up over time, along with how the organization can distribute them along the development process. At a minimum, a CFD contains three sections: **Backlog**, **In Progress**, and **Done**. Depending on the process, there might be five or six stages to any graph —as they transition from stage to stage, overall quantities with each category shift. The system has these shifts graphed over time, showing the shifting project status as the organization completes work.

A good project will have a smooth CFD from start to finish. Any roughness or random jumps in individual sections imply that the team should change something in its approach. One standard way of managing team output is actually through output restriction, using a **Work In Progress (WIP) limit**; this means that the team limits the number of projects developed at once.

That this tool exists should emphasize one crucial point: the goal of a Kanban process is not to thrash and complete a project as fast as humanly possible, exhausting a team and hurting morale. The hope is actually to maintain a fluent state of production—an efficient and effective rhythm for the longevity of a project. There is a set of tools and metrics that Kanban uses to achieve this rhythm.

New Toys: Metrics

Despite being a "sibling" of Scrum and other Agile system, Kanban uses a different set of metrics. Kanban has much of its foundation built for inventory management and manufacturing, making its parameters more similar to supply chain metrics than other Agile ideas.

Throughput: the total number of tasks completed in a measured amount of time.

Lead Time: the time a task spends on the board between existing and "Done."

Cycle Time: the time a task spends "In Progress."

Blocked Time: how long a card remains in a "blocked" state.

Wait Time: how long a card spends waiting on something.

Each of these metrics measures and records system waste that teams can avoid with continuous delivery. Because there is no set iterative timetable, the internal motivation of the team to keep these numbers competitive is typically the only real factor keeping them down. We will elaborate on this idea of picking the right people for a team in chapter eight.

Typically, a Kanban team will assess these metrics on a weekly or monthly basis. This means that organizations need to record the data consistently throughout that downtime. The entire methodology requires implementing recording systems, either physically or through various technologies and applications, more so than other Agile methods. When in Scrum, we can define success by delivering a complete set of products at the end of an iteration; Kanban does not have that luxury. However, by measuring the waste that results from a system, a team can eliminate it effectively.

Reducing waste in a Kanban system is one of the two core forces behind process improvement. Waste is the production time used ineffectively or unnecessarily. While every industry has waste, not every industry can address the root of the issue like software developers and other digital professionals. Kanban systematically engages in the fight to dissipate all seven categories of waste by using four different strategies.

1. Limiting Work Progress

Kanban focuses on the flow of projects—jerking around the CFD is terrible for the customer, production team, and any executives looking onward. The pull system allows for a smooth outflow of projects onto an individual that can handle it. But limiting work progress means limiting the entire team to only two or three tasks. Not only does this allow the team to focus its attention on the more complicated, longer-lasting tasks that may require multiple eyes, but it also reduces the number of defects by enabling organizations to take their time.

2. Visualizing

The horizontal progress bar broken down by tasks can be helpful to teams. Not only does it help with internal communication and allow a team to redistribute efforts as needed, but it also works to reallocate resources depending on the current reality. If excess cards exist somewhere, an organization can quickly recognize them and shift workloads where they are most needed.

3. Workflow Automation and Flexibility

Repetitive tasks will emerge in any project. These tasks can be either automated or eliminated, and flexibility of the team allows for a shift in focus toward all value-enhancing projects, including one that will enable the team to move forward.

4. Process Efficiency

The main reason why groups adopt Kanban methods is because their current team is barely meeting deadlines despite exceptional levels of stress and overtime. Kanban is known for reducing overall effort and reducing delivery time, so why not try it?

It's true! Kanban achieves quicker delivery dates and

less overall effort. How? It focuses on the efficiency of a project rather than the surrounding noise. Kanban is characterized by means of a critical metric: *flow efficiency*.

Flow efficiency is a measurement of the actual work time compared to waiting times in a single ratio. These are the two components that make up a team's lead time. Kanban's most effective measures of waste reduction come from reducing waiting time and improving this ratio! A team can measure flow accurately over a single iteration, but they are more likely to apply this ratio to the entire process. From that point, a team only needs two pieces of information from the list of metrics mentioned earlier: overall lead time and active work time. As overall lead time is equivalent to (work + waiting time), we can write the final ratio as:

$$Flow\ Efficiency\ \% \ = \ Work\ /\ (Work\ +\ Wait)\ *\ 100$$

If a team is working with a pull system and running an active board, they can find both numbers by measuring the movement of tasks on the board. They can track the precise time in each in small quantities, but they should define the waiting and work time beforehand. Measuring seconds can be more harmful than helpful. Discover what the right balance for the team is, as too much pressure placed on the members of the team by a measurement system typically leads to system abandonment. For units not measuring this critical metric, flow efficiency is often around 15%. In Kanbun systems, "good" is above 40%.

Independent of that massive jump in expectations regarding the team productivity, measuring this metric is an opportunity to address the customer's general satisfaction. Running an efficient team leads to a better product with a faster turnaround—it's a win-win! However, measuring may not provide an organization with answers for how to address the issue of waste. The first step to solving any problem is to understand that one exists—this metric provides the basis for constant improvements within the more extensive system. There are factors outside of the team that can drag that number down.

5. General Dependencies

These are typically shared services, either through specialists or a general vendor. But dependencies on one team may interrupt another team; a team may also become a source of dependency for another. The groups would address these dependencies early in the product architecture, so it is vital to explore safeguards. This can mean contacting and advising secondary specialists or vendors of a potential work opportunity early on.

6. Variation

The goal of a Kanban system is to achieve a smooth flow throughout the production cycle. Inevitably, given the work and variable makeup of a Kanban team, there will be encounters with tasks that are either more difficult or easier than initially expected. This results in a team attempting to understand the problem that it is working on rather than actually fix it. This queuing or buffering period is difficult to anticipate. Solutions start in the idle time allocated to each task—the more significant this amount is, the smoother the flow. However, there is a danger to allocating too much time to the various tasks, as this can take the pressure off the team and result in late project delivery.

Kanban teams are not cross-functional in the same way that a Scrum team is — the result is a list of specialists who are very good at their jobs. However, if a team only comprises back-end specialists, this will make front-end tasks take much longer. Organizations can address this during formation—the challenge that follows is assigning the right jobs to the right team members. The team is self-organizing, so it is crucial to relay strengths honestly and expose any misunderstandings concerning previous experience early on.

Chapter Seven Summary

- Kanban focuses on production as the restrictive factor and works to optimize it.
- It comes with a long list of new metrics, most of which are pulled directly from manufacturing practices (in Japan).
- Kanban focuses on optimizing flow efficiency more than any other metric.

The next chapter will look at the critical development of a team, answering the question: How do I build a team?

8

BUILDING AN ADAPTIVE TEAM

As diligent and close-to-perfect as a process can be, it is always in the service of a quality team. A good process will not magically make a bad Agile team functional. We can call any coordinated group of people working toward a shared goal a team. However, to be successful with Agile, said team must possess two specific qualities that go beyond the minimum definition: self-discipline and capability. Finding these people will make or break the entire project; beyond principles and rules, an Agile project is in the right, capable hands of the team involved. How can project managers find these critical figures?

The first step in building a team is understanding who to look for. Imagine the project manager as the head of a soon-to-be infamous heist. Maybe they need an explosives expert, a wheelman, an insider, and a hacker. Before they even approach the prospective employees, the organizer needs an exact idea of where each person goes into the project and how they will contribute to the achievement of the goal. Maybe they don't require a hacker for this project; a leader needs to understand that before they choose their team.

The same idea applies to Agile principles. When building a team, it is critical that the project manager has a clear idea of what skills, how many people, and other general boundary conditions a project may require. The importance of this analysis extends to the team once solidified. Connecting an individual to the project allows individuals within the organization to understand the relationship between roles. It further emphasizes the reason for specific drives and priorities within the project. Even if this may appear fine and dandy, there should exist a concise statement that allows all team members to connect instantly.

Creating a Vision

A compelling vision is the driving force behind successful projects. But why is it so often overlooked? Creating a compelling vision is very difficult; it requires work and leadership. Because the path forward is often intimidating and the best way not always clear, teams need something to guide them. This can, of course, be the leader who steps up in the face of intimidation, but the team must also be led on by a broader vision. There are four questions that a project manager needs to answer to develop a project vision:

1. What is the customer's product vision?
2. What are the scope and constraints of the project?
3. Who are the right participants to include in the project community?
4. How will the team deliver the product?

These questions should help define the project from a bird's-eye view. From there, a standard tool is the simple elevator pitch. This answers a few critical questions that act as a quick reference point for anyone who might need it. The **Elevator Pitch Test** is like a game of Mad Libs:

1. **For** [*target customer*]
2. **Who** [*needs this product/opportunity*]
3. **The** [*product name*] **is a** [*product category*]
4. **That** [*key benefits, reason(s) to buy*]
5. **Unlike** [*primary alternative*]
6. **Our Product** [*statement of differentiation*]

If the Elevator Pitch Test is not the best tool for a team, there is an alternative called the **Vision Box**. A vision box is a single piece of paper that acts as a constraint. The team would then be asked to describe the project in full, based on its most critical elements in the limited space available.

The beautiful thing about these tools is their informality, as none of them require anything else than a team and a manager's capabilities. The simplicity breathes through the entire project, from the first iteration to the last deployment. Once a project manager has defined the vision, the latter will lead them to the most appropriate team.

Project vision should never stop being articulated as the project evolves, as the better team members understands it, the better they can make trade-offs during day-to-day operations without interference. The product vision empowers the team and directly ties to individual investment—consistency in a message is key to morale. Not only is this a tool for finding the best team, but it is also a critical aspect of maintaining the enthusiasm for a project once the team has been created. From there, everything boils down to two infamous individual characteristics:

Self-discipline is an individual journey that an individual cannot force upon themselves. Some people can absorb the mentality of self-discipline quickly, while others take longer to instill it. Self-disciplined people accept accountability, confront reality, engage, work hard, and respect their colleagues. As a project manager, understanding where each individual lands with this skill ensures better team preparation. Consequences abound for the team who doesn't possess self-discipline. Imposed discipline undermines all the core values of Agile, leading to a complete crumble of the project and team. In Kanban systems specifically, which involve zero hierarchy, self-motivation and internal drive are critical for basic functionality.

We evaluate the second paramount skill potential team members as competence. More than skill and applicable knowledge, **competence** also refers to a person's attitude and experience. Competence is the fuel behind self-discipline—it enables intense discussions, a positive and respectful approach to other people, and trust within the team. Competence also comes with a level of honesty; when an individual properly understands their strengths and weaknesses, they better understand their place on the team. However, how does anyone know their position on a team when a team can remain undefined?

Self-organizing teams are not rambunctious, lawless groups of people marauding from project to project, nor are these teams leaderless or directionless. In a self-organized team, everyone manages their own workload. From there, organizations shift work around as they need and take part in larger decision-making. The reason for the importance placed on self-discipline is precisely this: the members of the team must trust one another to complete tasks.

This does not necessarily mean that there are no natural pressures within a team. Once a team grows in experience, both with each other and with customers, the evolution leads to certain expectations. Furthermore, there are media for investigation. Each daily scrum reports exactly what each person is working on over the course of the day—those who seem to be lagging are, therefore, exposed to the whole team and often the customer as well.

Agile Leadership

These are not leaderless teams; instead, they are characterized by the shift in leadership from a manager to a coach. We will elaborate on this idea in chapter nine, but the shift is deliberate and difficult to achieve. An Agile project manager is in the business of guiding people rather than correcting systems. Agile leaders empower the team, encourage interactions, and facilitate decisions. At their core, leaders show a team the questions they need to answer instead of answering for them. This shift in management style is a core aspect of a team's development and sustained success—it is the piece that links the system with the people. Agile employees have defined five ways for leaders to provide better services to teams:

1. Creating a Learning Culture

Self-organizing does not implicitly mean that a team is learning and growing personally. Ultimately, investment in the organization is an investment in the company. That begins and ends with welcome training with information concisely spread across multiple days' worth of Power-Points. Growing a learning culture within the team does not only allow the team to relax, but it also gives the highly skilled members a chance to explore something. Learning is not training; it is a chance for hands-on experimentation and working with new tools. Because the advances in modern technology are so rapid and widespread, the traditional sense of training around the emergence of new technologies is not enough. Employees need a chance to get their hands dirty with the things they want to learn, which will help them do their job better. Good leaders provide their employees with opportunities for personal growth.

2. Engaging employees in the transition

What makes a company attractive to a high-quality candidate? Is it bean bags and 401k matching? Specifically, in the modern American economy (but spreading to other corporate cultures), people are looking for opportunities in different roles. For high-quality candidates, pathways to professional and personal development are massive draws. As a company or project manager, one should rather focus on informing candidates of an impending promised change and engage them in the process. Rather than demanding employee loyalty to an idea or suggesting that movement is a recipe for failure, move employees to buy into the "why" of an organization's shift. This also requires vision from the leader, as he or she must communicate clearly.

3. Look beyond the spot market for talent

Project managers often run to HR with a list of positions, as if they were a grocery list, and ask, "How quickly can you find these people?" The HR manager will go to the broader "**Spot**" market, depending on hiring practices, and find a suitable candidate. They then process candidates, accept them, and finally welcome them to the team by having them work on a project as a new entry.

However, the perfect candidate could have been right under the management's nose the entire time. Because the hiring process is typically outwardly focused, the potential of internal hires is often overlooked. It is the job of leadership and management to make sure there are tools in place for helping internal personnel develop and making effective positions more biased in favor of experienced employees. Investments in recording and developing talents lead to happier employees—a consistent narrative.

4. Collaborate to deepen talent pool.

Aggressive efforts by companies to deepen talent pools create a tragedy of common [AC1] situations. Single companies usually swoop up as many employees as possible, but when every company does this, the result is a system that fosters a significant talent shortage. From a hiring perspective, it is in the best interest of companies to collaborate and work to understand how a few professionals can be efficiently distributed. Such an approach is not only beneficial for individual companies, but also for the "ecosystem" in which the companies co-exist and thrive.

5. Effort to managing chronic uncertainty though systematized flexibility

Modern businesses experience constant shifts in the business landscape—that fact is inescapable. However, there is a difference between externally generated uncertainty and internally developed uncertainty. The company's reaction to external uncertainty drives internal uncertainty—a rigidity within the company that requires more abrupt, dramatic shifts. This rigidity results in people losing jobs, staying where the organization doesn't need or want them and the overall burdening of the company.

Compare two businesses looking to adopt the best in class. One offers a position in a company with compelling growth potential, whereas the second offers a similar job with similar growth potential, but also horizontal access to other business units, projects, and opportunities. It is the difference between offering a child a ladder and a sandbox. A modern company's best chance of attracting and keeping talent is to constantly look elsewhere. Offer it all and enable the employee to give as much value to the company as possible.

Programs like this are not a novel idea. Large software companies have used internal platforms for volunteering on other teams, working on other projects, and developing experience in different business units for quite a while now. Not only does this flexibility empower and support the employee as their interests develop, but it also helps the company retain talent and remain efficient through the practical application of human capital. Other resources cannot organize themselves—they require management. People are very good at determining where they want to go, though, so it is best to create systems that allow your company's employees to self-organize. This support will reward you in full.

Finding the best team for the job is critical in all fields. But in an Agile project, it is the most crucial factor for success. Just as the ideas of management, project organization, and development have shifted with Agile systems, so must the arrangements for hiring and gaining talent. Given the current lack of developers and programmers in the field relative to demand, project managers need to understand that an unhappy employee can easily turn into a vacancy—

keeping team members happy also means keeping a project on track.

- Relying on traditional systems of hiring is not enough for hiring an Agile team.
- Employing a culture of learning and exploration to enable personal growth.
- Once employees are found, retaining them within the company walls is another challenge all together.

The next chapter will look at how management styles need to shift from traditional systems to Agile, leadership-driven ideals.

LEADERSHIP & COLLABORATIVE MANAGEMENT

Great leaders are standout figures throughout history. One was so "great" that the adjective became a part of his name in history books: Alexander the Great. Besides creating a big library, he never lost a battle, not one. Historians attribute this to many things—some say his father's wealth empowered him, or it was the strength of his cavalry. These may both be true, but one thing distinguished Alexander from all others, earning him his name in the history books: his leadership style.

The story of Alexander the Great's rise and battles with the Persian empire is ancient history in the effects of leadership against management. While the Persian king sat behind an army, directing and ordering as most generals did, Alexander fought side by side with his men. He would lead cavalry charges from the point of the spear, redirecting his armies within a moment's notice, overwhelming the opposing army. The men fighting under Alexander respected and valued him as their leader, literally following him into battle consistently. He constantly entrusted them with decision-making. Alexander lived outside of those moments. Beyond cultivating his army's respect through battlefield leadership, he was also a brilliant strategist, constantly looking forward to new opportunities before and after the chaos of a battle.

Though a modern Agile team has fewer spears and horses involved in their day-to-day lives, Alexander's lessons have been passed down for hundreds of years as an investigation of human character. From him, project managers can take more than a few lessons concerning inspiration, adaptation, and trust. This chapter will investigate how project managers can shift to project leaders.

From the Manager, a Leader Emerges

The first step to any social shift is a change in mindset. The mindset of a successful manager is suitable for management situations—it focuses on repairing and directing. The questions a reasonable manager asks are: "What are we doing to do about this problem?" and "What is the most efficient method to do this?" These are questions for a management situation, and they work fantastically! However, a self-organizing team does not technically require management; they are, by definition, *self-managing*. Agile methodologies inherently transfer those "what" questions to the responsibility of the group, no matter what type of chart or system is being used.

Even so, teams need a **leader**. Despite them being officially *leaderless,* they do require a figure to turn to in order to answer the "how" questions. "How are we going to approach this chronic issue?" or "How do we define success when being confronted with a difficult and demanding customer?" A leader asks the "how" questions, develops questions, and explores places unturned. They remain the guardian of the while guiding it gently by means of these development questions.

The problems the team asks the manager to address are immediate and contained within a more extensive system. The job of a manager is to manage an existing system—solutions typically found inside the system are beside the problems. But with an Agile method, the team and customers define the issues and solutions, and others already allocate the work within the existing system. So, how can a manager shift their mindset to become a relevant leader?

Leaders look beyond the current system rather than accepting reality as a base. This further shift in mindset provides a framework for constant improvement; questions in a gray area require the leader to make an effective decision. Because they are venturing into the unknown, a leader needs to step boldly with reassuring confidence, thus making it clear that their decision is the best.

Managers focus on risks within the current system; leaders focus on the outside. This allows the leader to reach into the outside world, bring people together through passion, create communities and movements that inspire, and ensure guidance for the team's efforts. Leaders check regularly and work to remove obstacles for their team. Everything about the mindset of a manager needs to switch —it is a challenging but attainable shift of perspective. This shift also includes the leader's attitude toward risk.

Risk within a project is a constant variable that the team will respect whether they recognize it. Risk management in any system means applying a set of ideals to ensure minimum risk with the maximum reward. The ability to stomach the risk and take on the burden falls to the manager. And because the manager has control over most of the existing system, the natural reaction is to reach towards risk management. Managers identify risks before they materialize due to their familiarity with the system. If a system is failing, managers act as a catalyst for change and repair. This is a precious element for most teams. And Agile teams, as with the other managerial jobs, have absorbed these risk management responsibilities.

A leader focuses on huge risks outside of the system. This can include anything from shifting customer tastes, introduction and adoption of disruptive technologies, or changes to relevant markets. The leader's first job is to filter critical shifts down to the team and allow them to take the appropriate measures. From there, a leader will work with the team to decide how to invest resources in combating risks. There is only one internal risk that a leader must address: team dynamics.

Team Dynamics

Team dynamics require a unique balanced approach to leadership. Returning to that Agile place is a strenuous process, and team dynamics are built on a foundation of trust and honesty. The erosion of trust and honesty in Agile teams does not come from lies or deception, but through the withholding of information. Withholding information will almost always lead to conflict and failure, for it undermines the core strengths of Agile forces.

There are two ways a person beats the famous game theory experiment called **The Prisoner's Dilemma**. Both parties must possess a religious faith that the other will not confess, or they need to communicate. While they can build trust over time, they rarely achieve the religious-faith level of trust within a single iteration. Communication is much easier for project teams than prisoners, so why is information ever withheld? It can be for many reasons: fear, a lack of understanding regarding potential ramifications, or even a slip of the mind. Leaders cannot solve the problem by addressing the many roots, but by leading a team to a sustainable solution.

Collaboration uproots the prisoner's dilemma and is the core of every Comm 101 class. It is described it through the four stages of cooperation: **forming**, **storming**, **norming**, and **performing**. These four phases act as the natural life cycle of a collaborative system, slowly bending teams together and allowing the chronic problem of withholding information to evaporate. Where withholding information is a shadow, collaboration is the sun that completely banishes it. While these stages [AC1] will contribute to community unity and trust, there may be personal differences that impede the power of collaboration.

Teams often avoid disagreeing for fear of conflict. Managers take to the system for a solution, relying on internal structures to be respected and upheld, constructing and using conflict resolution skills and processes, and ultimately brokering the peace or final resolution. Do not avoid conflict. Instead, express it constructively in a resolution system. The strength of this system directly impacts the number of times a team uses it instead of resorting to withholding information, so it cannot survive as an afterthought. Withheld information is usually personal differences within the confines of the organization, but what happens if conflict originates with parties outside the sphere of influence?

Resolving conflict with external actors falls upon the leader's shoulders. Before attempting to remedy a problem, leaders must first work to identify and understand the basis of the conflict with customers, suppliers, or partners. With the effectiveness of the team at stake, there is no time to beat around the bush—a leader must quickly and directly seek conflict to resolve it. More than something to fix, a conflict is a rare opportunity to develop a deeper bond with an external figure.

Leaders and managers both have their places in an Agile team. Even if the self-organizing team has absorbed many of the manager's responsibilities, the leader is as relevant as ever. Regardless of who guides the process, modern units are turning toward one popular tool for organizing.

Application Performance Management (APM)

Application Performance Management, or **Application Performance Monitoring** (**APM**), is a form of active, ongoing management, which manifests itself in measuring performance, availability, and end-user experience software. The goal of APM is to shift from the customer ordering a project to the actual end-users, ensuring the customer's satisfaction indirectly. With the availability of data and continually connected end-users, technology has made this development a reality. Within APM, there are five core tools that ensure functionality:

1. End-User Experience Monitoring (EUM)
2. Runtime Application Architecture Discovery Modeling and Display
3. User-defined Transaction Profiling
4. Component Deep Dive Monitoring
5. Analytics

Collectively, these allow a developer or IT department to constantly monitor the activity of an application or system. They enable rapid solution deployment to critical issues, and prioritize other matters as needed.

APM is typically used for massive, internally developed

consumer applications like Uber or Wells Fargo Mobile Banking to substitute a lack of third-party support industry. But the system has expanded to any customer-facing software, including both general webpages and e-commerce stores. So, what if an IT group were to apply APM principles to internal problems?

Internally, applications and technology are the tools that run companies. Every department, from sales and supply chain to human resources, is reliant upon these applications. Why not treat them as internal end-users and have the team act as if it were investigating for a client? The results can be more than impressive:

Increase in Sales

A modern sales manager is half man, half **customer relationship management** (**CRM**) system. When the CRM is running slow, failing, or not functioning properly, it costs the company productive time and potentially closed sales. These critical systems exist throughout companies in every department.

This is only internally focused, as well! In a B2C situation, a customer who cannot access a website or sales page is most likely not going to return for a second attempt.

When an entity uses APM principles that display architecture and issues in real-time, it can quickly address any problems that dare present themselves.

End User Experience

Forcing a team's attention to the end-user experience at every step of the process shifts modern IT teams from engineers to business minds. We can apply business metrics with end-user experience that defines effectiveness and prioritization, and the systems will improve. This is in part due to the measurement of the priorities.

Improved IT Productivity

As another factor of those new metrics, IT teams can prioritize time and energy in line with general demand.

Exploration

Beyond new systems like APM, a common theme in successful Agile is learning. Self-organizing does not mean self-learning or self-development. A leader must facilitate the development and growth of a team. Because exploration is considered the most effective form of learning, these learning and growth sessions are promoted through exploration days.

An exploration day is a day of complete freedom. As a leader, you can dedicate a day or two to employee personal projects. Restrictions are typically minimal, working only to foster a learning environment that nudges employees to explore. For the uninspired, here is a list of events that empower employee exploration:

1. Have a Hackathon
2. Organize a Book Club
3. Plan a Personal Growth Consultation
4. Visit Conferences
5. Build communities of practice
6. Visit other companies
7. Slack off

These are designed mostly to allow team members to

run free and explore a burning idea or itch a question they might be holding on to. So, have fun! Schedule time to explore, learn, and grow. As the leader, use this as an effort to take care of those dependent on your good judgment.

Chapter Nine Summary

- Leadership is about guiding and empowering rather than directing and managing risks.
- New ideas like APM are constantly emerging— be aware of the shifting world around the team.
- Sew growth and learning into a team through scheduled explorations.

In the next chapter, we will explore the most common reasons for Agile project failure will be explored in depth.

COMMON ERRORS BEHIND AGILE FAILURE

Just as Agile methodology comes in many forms and flavors, so do its failures. While Agile projects typically have a much lower failure rate than their WaterFall counterparts, unsuccessful projects still happen; these are defined by a lack of delivered projects, insufficient customer satisfaction, exaggerated expense, or carelessly allotted calendar space. The reasons behind these failures have a pattern to them, typically stemming from four fundamental issues within a team or organization. The reasons for these failures are a critical lack of support, broader organization or communication problems, project speed, or inadequate training. If a team can overcome, prevent, or reinvent around these four problems while running authentic Agile, the project has an infinitely better chance of landing a stamp of approval from each stakeholder involved.

Lack of Support

As we have already established in previous chapters, organizing a support structure behind an Agile team is the core functionality of a project manager. This means giving power and decision-making authority to a group of professional programmers rather than following a more traditional hierarchy. Organizations can achieve this through executive buy-in at the highest level—if the CEO of a company pledges their unwavering support to the efforts of an Agile team, they often have little trouble parting the sea of corporate bureaucracy.

However, this support means more than gracing a team with the leader's presence at the start of a project. Agile projects need resources and funding upfront, two things that executives control. They also need access to information and people, two more things that executives control. Executive buy-in means granting reasonable access to the things the team needs to complete the project on time and budget, and then trusting them to handle the resources with care.

A common expression of this pitfall is underwriting executive support to another person without proper authority. A local manager may grant access to rooms and whiteboards, but they cannot allow a significant hardware investment within one iteration. Furthermore, they do not represent the support of an executive team, which is arguably more critical than resource allocation. The fastest way to have a project fail is to have an executive kill it. Period. If someone on the executive team does not clue in to the real vision and impact of the project on the customer and the benefits for the company, they can get in the way and sabotage the entire effort, reducing weeks or months of a team's effort to nothing.

Even though this may seem extreme, you need to understand that Agile practices often threaten the internal culture of a company—hierarchical and traditional in exchange for something more spontaneous. This cultural shift directly threatens the executives' power structure, specifically affecting those who act as managers rather than leaders. Beyond shifts in the organization's direction, disorganization and a lack of respect for the process, some executives may think their jobs, position, status, and identity are being threatened. Undermining the efforts of an Agile team, especially a new one, is, therefore, in their best interest. This manifests in support for a WaterFall method and a company philosophy, which is at odds with the Agile methodology.

Look for an executive looking outside the organization and toward the future and prosperity of the company. They will see the value of Agile in a rapidly changing world as an opportunity rather than a threat. At some point, projects and efforts become political within a big enough company— leave this piece to the executives supporting a team's efforts instead of focusing on it more than necessary.

Broader Organizational or Communication Issues

As unique and independent as Agile teams may feel once inside, they still operate within the larger organizational space. Systemic weaknesses negatively affect all parts of the systems, no matter how Agile. These are much larger, organization-specific issues that the team must consider before implementing an Agile project system. Is the organization culturally ready to accept a shift to a more independent framework? Will those outside the Agile team readily accept or outright reject it? Are the communication systems in place strong enough to support the demands of an Agile team?

There are things a project manager can do to address these questions and the many more that, if left unanswered, may undercut the efforts of an Agile team. One of these is executive buy-in, as mentioned previously, but general buy-in can be just as critical. Involving mid-tier managers by keeping them informed, asking what questions they might have about the process, and understanding huge reservations is key to breaking the ice of a project. Moreover, it leads to an understanding of the Agile team's demands, communication, or requests for information. Poor communication is seldom malicious at this level, preferably an initial miscommunication of important information. To prevent that or other problems that may arise externally, you should include them in conversations early in the process, explaining their significance in the functionality of the team's success.

A more robust method, especially for a team starting with an Agile process, is to create a level of value for those teams and engage them in the system's success. Organizations typically apply Agile methods to software and development projects, but as explored in past chapters, they have a wide range of applications beyond those worlds. If a manager has never heard of Agile practices, speak with them about it, and see where those principles may fit into their world. From there, test principles within the first Agile team and report back to the manager: "This worked, that was a problem, these are the solutions I used." Not only does this engage the rest of the organization with the individual project, but it also works to "infect" the culture of an organization with a single suggestion: there may be a better, newer way to approach organizational problems. From there, the organizational culture loosens and becomes open to addressing the issues of a system more broadly.

Going Too Fast

The move to an Agile system, especially if it carries the expectation of a "solution to all our problems," can be exciting. While jumping into Agile unprepared is a bad idea, speeding through the process is just as dangerous. Often, issues of speed management stem from poor coaching, processes, or tooling. These core issues present themselves in three flavors:

1. Not defining a process to absorb issues regarding multiple dependent or distributed teams

Defining a project without the entire consideration of all relevant stakeholders undermines effectiveness. However, Agile teams can often work around this oversight with executive authority or team restructuring. If a dependent squad has not been adequately accounted for, it halts the entire progression of a project, ripping through the process like a malfunctioning crane on an assembly line. If a team does not define a method for addressing this potential fault before it begins, it becomes, by definition, impossible to move forward and continue the project. Often, a desire to rush into a project creates this oversight, which is the result of little consideration rather than lack of foresight—take the time to build the structures a project needs to succeed.

2. Scalability issues with core Agile tools

"Give me six hours to chop down a tree, I will spend the first four sharpening the axe."

Though this quote is often wrongly attributed to Abraham Lincoln, the wisdom encapsulated by it extends into the software development world through Agile implementation. Agile tools are designed to automate and support larger systems; they act as a strength multiplier just as the axe does. When developing tools to help a broader functionality, we might be tempted to jump straight to the functionality rather than further invest in the tools themselves. The rush to produce often produces a base tool, which becomes inaccessible after its first use. Do not rush through the fundamental development of tools for the sake of production—this will cause more retooling down the line or, worse, a functionality that does not live beyond a development tool and results in failed implementation. Furthermore, team members must use tools consistently. The inconsistent use of a tool can cause faulty metrics, overall incorrect builds, and flow or quality issues.

3. Extending tools to the wrong processes like testing or business collaborations

Retooling and artifacts are the key to making an Agile system even more efficient; however, that mindset leads to the temptation to reuse tools inappropriately for the sake of speed and convenience. Extending a means to address issues it was not built for, such as a general deployment, testing, or other business collaborations, may cause a more significant failure down the line, when proper tools are finally in place. This is a small detail that often causes a lot of havoc within an Agile team. Proper retooling usually means recoding and an in-depth understanding of a tool's more substantial functionality; as a project manager, encourage an Agile team to ask, "In what ways can this tool be better for this application?" before reusing a tool, then retool it based on the answer.

Teams do all of this by experiencing pressure and

cutting corners because speed is the focus, not quality. Finding the balance between speed and quality is never easy, but consistently undercutting quality for the sake of speed is a critical ingredient in the Agile project failure soup.

Poor Training

Insufficient training is a common reason for failure, which occurs in three forms: nobody receives training, not everyone who needed it got it, or the training wasn't great. While the first two can be solved through proper scheduling, the third directly results from having a poor coach. Why is finding qualified Agile coaches so tricky? Many people are unsure of what to look for in an Agile coach. And this goes beyond trusting a certification, history, or experience.

The first strategy is through formal training experience. Within the software community, there are loose definitions attached to programs or people themselves. A "software developer" might be someone who attended a graduate program, and developed skills in years of practice with complicated problems and projects. Then, there are self-taught, new hires, whose experience consists of a few personal projects and a cluster of YouTube videos. While an inexperienced software developer can still develop good software and often find new and unique ways to do so, a coach does not have that luxury. The Agile coach needs to experience coaching and being coached over the years to be effective.

The first step to clearing a coach is to get references and understand how deeply their experience extends. This applies both to coaching and Agile skills independently. Apprenticeship under another Agile coach is a great way to establish these skills, though there are a variety of legitimate Agile coaching organizations available. These organizations not only focus on how to coach Agile specifically, but they go deep into Agile skills and knowledge. This leads to a second requirement.

An Agile coach knows Agile. This seems like an obvious requirement, but a coach may claim to know Agile without truly understanding the principles. Years of experience do not guarantee a deep understanding of all aspects of the Agile Lifecycle. Delivering an excellent coaching experience means coaching all parts of a team, including enterprise architecture, data management, and portfolio management.

Finally, an Agile coach should have experienced a context that is similar to an organization's project. This not only applies for the project, but also for organizational realities. Coaching a team that is centrally located and coaching a team from a different time zone on the globe are two different experiences. Even clearer is the difference between a modern startup whose team might include the majority of the company's personnel and a large organization in which the team is barely a percentage of the company's payroll. A good Agile coach should have sufficient experience in any given context, or at least possess transferable knowledge that he or she can apply to specific situations. Context is relevant.

By following these steps, you will ensure that the common pitfalls of Agile implementation and management are avoided successfully. Good luck!

Chapter Ten Summary

- Finding the right executive to buy into a project

directly impacts the functionality of that
project.

- Take the time to build the structures upfront or
suffer the consequences later.
- Coaches are critical—vet them like any high-
ranking employment.

FINAL WORDS: AGILE IS ADAPTATION

Every Agile project manager that ventures with a project into the world is driven by a desire to solve complicated problems. There is also a broader dissatisfaction regarding the way we address new challenges with old methods, though.

Agile is the modern way to address current problems. The reality accompanying the 21st century is one of constant deployment, innovation, and technological shifts. It affects every industry, from news and fashion to B2B companies. Companies are faced with a question—resist the wave or learn to ride it to shore. For many problems, Agile management acts as the surfboard that allows you to navigate this crazy, fungible world.

The data are there to support the core processes of Agile methods. The software world has extensively analyzed the difference between traditional, hierarchical approaches and dynamic, Agile ones. As it turns out, 86% of conventional projects are failures. About half of those failures produce no working software and zero product delivery. The people involved in the system demanded a radical change, and Agile was the response.

Not only does Agile produce a final product more often by reducing the failure rate to under 10%, but it also increases the quality of delivered projects. This happens systematically, as the relevance of a project to the overall system is no longer determined by shifts in the external environment. This reorientation from determination to adaptation is highly critical. If the project requirements change, it is up to the project team to shift with them. Agile management allows for that shift to be systematic, thus encouraging and developing applications that are relevant to the end-user.

An Agile approach also ensures higher customer satisfaction. Incorporating a customer in the development process introduces aspects of accountability with buy-in. The level of customer interaction in Agile settings allows teams to evolve with the demands, threading the needle between consistency and flexibility. Overall, there are significantly more chances to make sure the customer is happy. It's as simple as that!

There is also a gripping sense of control that comes with Agile. It stems from the way a team organizes its work. Work is not a list of process requirements and neither does it involve dictating terms and directing an entire team through the descriptions of a document. It verbalizes the complaints from the mouth of the only person who matters: the customer. Rather than handing in a to-do list, the customer pleads with the team to help them. They provide constraints and a problem. From there, it is up to the team of experts to determine the most effective solution and implement it. Agile provides room for expertise, nuance, and creativity to become assets rather than risks. This is a powerful shift for both the customer and the team, motivating each to be diligent and inquisitive rather than working to deliver a list.

The metrics show all of this too. Not only do Agile approaches reduce the risk of project failure, but they also create a faster ROI for the company and customers alike. Agile projects commonly come under-budget and ahead of schedule. With the disparity in quality also accounted for, what more could a system provide? Agile methodologies are better for modern problems that require iterative problem solving and solutions.

These benefits would be bare offerings without the methods, allowing incorporation into the companies. Agile methods rely on a few core tenets: planning, communication, and team development.

The foundation of an Agile system is the people within it. In a world of automation and computerization, Agile methods are uniquely, perhaps ironically, human. The shift from a hierarchy-driven organization to a self-organizing team, with its power and structure, is a challenge to overcome. It requires leadership rather than management, executive support, and internal determination. But from that shift comes the rest—it is the effort to see the field that begets the benefits.

Shifting from plan to planning is often the most challenging step for one reason—it's the first step. The initial instinct of every traditional organization is to develop a concrete plan; shifting that perspective is a cumbersome task, for you also need to move the accompanying organizational inertia. But the benefits outweigh the apparent disadvantages, because in exchange for the effort you get an adaptable, functional team that continually betters and evolves.

That is, unless poor communication squanders those efforts. In a traditional organization, money is the blood that leads to project success. With Agile projects, it is information. Apart from internal, functional communication, there is a communication of vision that needs to take place. Most jobs don't require sustained buy-in and commitment, but Agile projects do. The only accurate way to do that is by inspiring the right people.

This book provided a bird's-eye view into the world of Agile. But there is much more to dive into, should you choose to adopt this approach. Not only are there more in-depth investigations of how we apply Agile, but there are also more ways and systems where we could use Agile methods. Each Agile system has its nuances. As we saw in the chapter about Scrum and Kanban and the portion on ALM, we can use each application with diverse problems and ensure success. Finding a system that works best for each company is a matter of education and consultation. Hopefully, this book introduced you to a few questions and terms that you can use.

Apart from terminology and questions, this book also introduced a critical idea: complex, **modern** problems demand **modern** systems. There is no quick answer or set of rules to change. These problems will not go away with excessive working hours or dollars. They are problems that demand a **modern** solution—a system—to address them. They require a shift in perspective and understanding rather than resources. That shift needs to be malleable, in line with the times, and easy to reorganize when called upon for a different problem. It is a high bar to satisfy our modern times. But thankfully, Agile systems allow us to do just that.

THANK YOU

First of all, thank you for purchasing this book - **Agile Project Management: A Beginner's Guide to Agile Implementation and Leadership**. *I know you could have picked any other book to read, but you have picked this one, and for that I am extremely grateful.*

If you enjoyed this book and found some benefit in reading it, I'd like to hear from you. I hope that you could take some time to post a review on Amazon. Your feedback and support will help this author to greatly improve his writing craft for future projects, thus making this book even better.

Printed in Great Britain
by Amazon